JUL 1 4 2000		
	JUL 2 7 2000		
	AUG 2 5 2000		
	MAY 1 6 2003		

The New England
BUTT'RY SHELF ALMANAC

The New England
BUTT'RY SHELF
ALMANAC

being a Collation of Observations on
New England People, Birds, Flowers,
Herbs, Weather, Customs, and Cookery
of Yesterday and Today

MARY MASON CAMPBELL

ILLUSTRATED BY

TASHA TUDOR

THOMAS Y. CROWELL COMPANY

NEW YORK · ESTABLISHED 1834

Copyright © 1970 by The World Publishing Company
All rights reserved
Library of Congress Catalog Card Number: 76-128491
Printed in the United States of America
Published in Canada by
Fitzhenry & Whiteside Limited, Toronto
ISBN 0-690-00361-7

2   3   4   5   6   7   8   9   10
The author and editor gratefully acknowledge
Imogene Wolcott, author of The Yankee Cook Book
published by Ives Washburn, Inc., for giving permission
to reprint the Christopher LaFarge verse,
"Rhode Island Clambake"; also Little, Brown and Company,
publishers of The Complete Poems
of Emily Dickinson, for cooperation.

POSIES

FOR MY

Mother

ALSO BY
MARY MASON CAMPBELL
ILLUSTRATED BY
TASHA TUDOR

The New England
BUTT'RY SHELF COOKBOOK

The Collation

COLOR ILLUSTRATIONS

The Almanac

All sorts of things and weather
Must be taken in together,
To make up a year
And a Sphere.
—RALPH WALDO EMERSON

ON A HANDWROUGHT iron hook embedded in the brown pine face-boards of the kitchen fireplace hung one of the indispensable aids to late eighteenth- and nineteenth-century New England households. The almanac brought life, humor, knowledge, and a prescience of things to come to all those forebears whose well-being often depended on it.

The early almanacs predicted the weather in the year ahead with abundant confidence, and to New Englanders the weather was of greatest importance. Enoch Little, who built his house in the hills of New Hampshire in 1791 and kept a diary each day of his life thereafter, commented on the weather before he mentioned weddings, births, deaths, barn-raisings, or church attendance. Not only did the almanacs predict the weather, but they gave ample advice to their readers for figuring out their own weather predictions.

Other useful information filled the pages of the almanacs, including rising and setting times of the moon and sun and planets; dates of court meetings and holidays; short homilies, the most famous of which were those which Benjamin Franklin inserted in his *Poor Richard's Almanack*, most of them being advice on morals and thrifts. Poetry was often included, puzzles and anagrams, advice on household management, and much other material providing reading and food for thought for the many long winter evenings ahead. Almanacs patterned after the old ones are still consulted with interest today, although they generally serve more for entertainment than practical use to the household.

It is easy to picture the scene at the fireside of any New England home in generations gone by, after supper dishes were put away and the family was busy with its evening tasks of spinning or winding bobbins, or cracking nuts, or whittling pegs for a new barn. It was probably father, or one of the youngsters going to the village school, who read aloud to the family such pages of weather and calendar interest as would be useful for the morrow. A puzzle or two would be solved and a poem read. Then the almanac would be hung on its hook and the Bible, the other all-important book, brought out for a reading of suitable verses before the family went to bed.

Usually almanacs hung on their hook for several years, the latest one on top, and were used until they became dog-eared and brown. The booklets were then stacked on the shelf of the butt'ry where the cooking receipts were kept, and for many years afterward the rules contained in their pages were tried and used for reference, until at last the booklets were stored away in the attic, for they might come in handy again someday.

In a gentle mood of nostalgia, *The New England Butt'ry Shelf Almanac* has been written in the hope that it, too, will furnish interesting and useful information to all those who love New England, its customs and people, its old houses and ghosts, its hills and valleys and rivers and coves, and its ways of keeping house and garden.

Warm thanks are herewith given to all those before me who contributed to the preparation of this *Almanac* in ways they could not have foreseen. Thanks, too, to Sayles Gorham and Dr. Nicholas Gorham for recollections and stories; to Ruth Sawyer for sharing with me her ancestors' diaries; to the gracious ladies of the Providence Athenaeum, the Vermont

Historical Society, and the Wickford Public Library; to Barbara Bruening of the Glastonbury, Connecticut, Historical Society; Gretchen Tobey of the New Hampshire Historical Society; John Dunn of the state of New Hampshire Library; the girls in Congressman James A. Cleveland's office in Washington for help in locating material in the Library of Congress; Lothian Lynas of the New York Botanical Garden Library; Virginia MacLeod and James A. Conlon, director of the U. S. Treasury Department Bureau of Engraving and Printing, for help in identifying with certainty Gilbert Stuart data. My thanks to Ginette de Rabaudy of Senlis, France, for teaching me how to make her French Onion Soup, which induced my husband to relish eating onions for the first time in his life; to my sister Evelyn Watters, and to Gillian Murphy, Margaret Whitlatch, and Etta Scott for special receipts; to Maud Prince for a delightful visit on New England's ways of predicting weather; to Mittie Arnold and Margaret Thomas of the Greene Herb Gardens for their help and encouragement. And especial thanks for *many* things to Tasha, Ruth, Sis, and Douglas.

MARY MASON CAMPBELL

The Farm
Salisbury, New Hampshire

The New England
BUTT'RY SHELF ALMANAC

Wedding Anniversaries

First	Paper	*Thirteenth*	Lace
Second	Cotton	*Fourteenth*	Ivory
Third	Leather	*Fifteenth*	Crystal
Fourth	Flowers	*Twentieth*	China
Fifth	Wood	*Twenty-fifth*	Silver
Sixth	Candy	*Thirtieth*	Pearl
Seventh	Copper	*Thirty-fifth*	Coral
Eighth	Bronze	*Fortieth*	Ruby
Ninth	Pottery	*Forty-fifth*	Sapphire
Tenth	Tin	*Fiftieth*	Gold
Eleventh	Steel	*Fifty-fifth*	Emerald
Twelfth	Silk	*Seventy-fifth*	Diamond

Monday's child is fair of face,
Tuesday's child is full of grace,
Wednesday's child is loving and giving,
Thursday's child works hard for a living.
Friday's child is full of woe,
Saturday's child has far to go,
But the child that is born on the Sabbath-day
Is brave and bonny, and good and gay.

JANUARY

Birthstone and Birthdays

January's Birthstone is the *Garnet*, which means *Constancy*.

1	16
2	17
3	18
4	19
5	20
6	21
7	22
8	23
9	24
10	25
11	26
12	27
13	28
14	29
15	30
	31

Flower

THE FLOWERING ALMOND
Amygdalus

IT WAS a charming custom in the nineteenth century to give meanings to flowers. In this way, a young man could express his sentiments to his lady love simply by giving her a flower; or if he was overflowing with admiration, he could speak a long piece by giving her a bouquet. Friends could exchange greetings by their exchange of posies, and even expressions of sympathy, congratulation, or esteem could be indicated. The special meaning of January's flower, the Almond, was *Hope*.

> The hope in dreams of a happier hour,
> Which alights on misery's brow,
> Springs out of the silvery almond flower,
> That blooms on a leafless bough.
>   —SARAH JOSEPHA HALE

The Almond is a shrub native to the Eastern countries, particularly China. It flowers very early before its leaves appear, and its blossoms are pink or white. It was found in old-fashioned gardens of New England, and still blooms beside doorways of many colonial houses.

Bird

THE BLACK-CAPPED CHICKADEE
Parus atricapillus

THE state bird of Maine and Massachusetts is my affectionate choice for January's bird, the Black-capped Chickadee. This irrepressibly gay little bird brightens the long New England winters with its cheerful "chickadee-dee-dee" call as it darts in and out of bird-feeders, pine trees, and shrubs, like a diminutive flying acrobat of some circus-of-the-air. He seems to feel a great responsibility in spreading good cheer during the winter, for he is at his gayest during the stormiest days.

A Chickadee's life span is about nine years, which seems a long time for such a tiny creature. It is one of the most useful of birds, as it consumes great quantities of cankerworms, moths, and their eggs, and weed seeds as well. Sunflower seeds in the feeder never fail to attract the busy fellow. With dexterity and skill, he grasps a seed in his bill, then flies to a nearby perch, holds the seed secure on the perch with one claw and hammers at the seed with his bill until the shell is broken. His busy wings in flight move almost as rapidly as those of a hummingbird.

The Chickadee inhabits various kinds of woodlands, seeming to prefer the shelter of evergreens in winter; but when it is time to nest, he is found in any densely timbered area. During the spring courting season and in summer, the Chickadee's call may be a rather wistful whistled note which sounds very much like the "pheebee" call of the phoebe bird. The female lays from six to ten eggs and usually has two broods a year.

It is not difficult to train a Chickadee to take sunflower seeds from an outstretched hand if one is willing to be patient and stand quietly at their feeding times. Once they are attracted to the feeders, they should be fed until springtime for they then are dependent on the feed provided for them.

The Chickadee could be a good example to us if we would but follow his behavior. His manners are exemplary. He eats daintily and is patient with other birds. He is cheerful on bright days, and just as cheerful and happy when the weather is dreary or stormy. He takes whatever we wish to give him in the way of food and shelter in winter, repaying amply with a melodious song of thanks and a happy disposition. In the spring, he minds his own business and goes off into the green woods to enjoy the quiet and the responsibilities of housekeeping without making any demands of us.

Piped a tiny voice hard by,
Gay and polite, a cheerful cry—
Chic-chicadeedee! saucy note
Out of sound heart and merry throat,
As if it said, "Good-day, good sir!
Fine afternoon, old passenger!
Happy to meet you in these places
Where January brings few faces."
—RALPH WALDO EMERSON

Our Old and Faithful Friend

Shut in from all the world without,
We sat the clean-winged hearth about. . . .
                    —JOHN GREENLEAF WHITTIER

THE earth is blanketed in white. We watch the full January moon rise over
the East Field, the bright light reflected as on ocean waves. Stone walls and
solitary rocks and bushes are crested with snow. And ice. Pine trees under
their meringue of white bow their heads and limbs, and within their depths
shelter the sleeping winter birds. Every branch of every tree and bush is
encased in crystal and shines in the blue winter moonlight like a prism. We
stand in awed wonder at the end of the lane, and listen to the silence. A
twig snaps, its burden of snow and ice too much to bear, and falls to the
ground, making the silence seem deeper. For January is a month of quiet.

The garden is asleep in its featherbed of deep snow, and I think prac-
tically of the nitrogen which will be so generously released to the plants and
the lawn when spring comes and the snows melt across the land. A New
Englander, Ralph Waldo Emerson, expressed it poetically:

> Over the winter glaciers
> I see the summer glow
> And through the wild-piled snowdrifts
> The warm rose-buds below.

Buds of apple blossom and lilac and rose are tight, showing no urge
to swell in the brief winter light. A cocoon shows plainly in the moonlight,

hanging from a branch of the forsythia bush. If a bird doesn't find it in his hunger, we must remember to remove it before warm days come.

The village is asleep, there is no light in any window along the country road which traverses it. No owl hoots in the moonlight; no dog barks; no train is heard in the keen night. Everything is serene. January is serene in the New England countryside. Except . . .

Except on a stormy night when the bitter blowing shafts of north wind howl in the chimney and whistle around the windows. Snow drifts through the cracks under the doorsill from the windswept yard, it piles against the old house. Steddy barks frantically as the snowplow goes roaring past in the raging storm. Then January is not quiet.

In the Old Kitchen we build a crackling fire of long-burning maple logs fed with birch for extra heat. The dooryard shrubs scratch insistently with icy fingers at the windowpanes. An occasional back-draft from the chimney blows a puff of wood smoke into the room and we appreciate its fragrance and its warmth.

Books are piled on the tables, in the corners, and on bookshelves, awaiting January nights like this. There are books of history, of biography and adventure; books on cookery; books on gardening, and one on greenhouse gardening, which we dream over and hope to make use of someday. There are new seed catalogs; and old books gathered all year long from odd corners of New England antique and old book shops. There are back numbers of magazines for which there never seemed to be time enough during the busy days of preceding months. They are all stacked here, waiting.

Since winter provides the time for garden planning for the spring, books by a favorite garden writer of the turn of the century, Gertrude Jekyll, are near at hand. Miss Jekyll didn't begin gardening in earnest until she had reached middle age, but she more than made up for lost time, and her facile pen provided a wealth of valuable as well as delightful reading. I have a collection of her books and in admiration and zeal have managed to acquire two copies of some of them. There is also among them a recently published anthology of her works prepared by Elizabeth Lawrence.

Miss Jekyll deplored the too-neat ribboned borders of the Victorian era in which she lived, and devoted much of her writing to naturalistic gardens and perennial borders as we know them today. She loved wild flowers. And she spent many happy hours searching out old-fashioned garden flowers from the country dooryards of England. Her advice and thoughts seem more timely today than they did during her own time.

In her book called *Flower Decoration in the House,* I find ideas and suggestions for arrangements which suit me and my two-hundred-year-old house and old-fashioned country garden. I often wonder what she would have thought of the self-conscious flower arranging that is done today in many American homes. Generally flowers well chosen arrange themselves most charmingly with a little encouragement, especially in an old house; they don't really have to be wired or cut to bits or dyed or enhanced with a piece of tree long dead, symbolic as that may be in Japan. Somehow in an old American house a simple bowl of field daisies or sweet peas or a single floating peony or a spray of clematis look very much at home without much arranging.

Some of our garden planning in January will certainly include a special corner for herbs, perhaps even an eighteenth-century version of a kitchen dooryard herb garden. And so with pencil and paper we toy with plans for a garden containing some of the most frequently used kitchen and fragrant herbs: chives, parsley, thyme, tarragon, chervil, sage, lovage, the mints, fennel, basil, marjoram, lavender, savory, dill, and lemon balm. The plan will include rosemary, some of the scented-leaved geraniums, lemon verbena, and heliotrope—these in pots as they are not winter-hardy.

There are many possibilities for herb gardens. They can be created with special attributes of fragrance, such as a Garden for the Blind; or of literary interest—a Shakespeare Garden or a Poets' and Dreamers' Garden; or of special use—a Tea Garden or a Dye or Kitchen Garden. There are Bible Gardens and Bee Gardens; Potpourri, Thyme, and Mint Gardens. Designs may be of wheels or ladders or wreaths or knots, or something suitable to the available space.

We reach back into the history of gardening and design a simple "knot garden" in the sixteenth-century manner and an intriguing pattern, then discard it in favor of an informal practical idea better adapted to the planting of miscellaneous herbs. An old wrought-iron, Shaker-made trivet suggests a lovely design, but we finally choose a wheel effect as being simple to construct and easy to maintain. The rim will be edged with a double row of old bricks, and so will the spokes. It could be edged with shells or small rocks with equal success. In the center will be a sundial.

Within the rim of bricks, parsley and chervil in alternating ribbons will surround the entire garden, and between the spokes of the brick wheel will be placed our favorite herb plants. We make a list of seeds to buy and write out the order for them now, for starting on the windowsill in February or March; and another list of plants to buy, such as tarragon which must be started from cuttings, and other perennials. We begin the whole list with angelica, which we candy and use for decorating cakes and cookies at Christmas, and puddings any time of the year. It grows tall, likes damp shady places and so will be planted under the trees in the old orchard rather than within the wheel, as will the mints.

Herb gardens can be planned so as to require a minimum of maintenance, be easy to reach from the kitchen door, be of handsome appearance and delightful smell. There should be a surprise or two—perhaps a stone figure of a frog or squirrel, or an old-fashioned straw bee skep, or an ancient pottery water jug, or a johnny-jump-up seedling in its own chosen spot. Space for a small wooden or stone bench should be planned somewhere nearby, the better to enjoy the sight and fragrance of such a treasure garden.

This fragrance is particularly delightful in early morning or evening, or on a damp day. I like to have a pot of rose geraniums or lemon verbena or heliotrope beside the door-rock, too, so that I can brush my hand over it lightly as I pass, just for the pleasure of the fragrance.

Among the old cookbooks which I love to pore over time and again is the delightful *Housekeepers' Book* published anonymously by "a lady" in Philadelphia in 1838. The title page of this book reads "Advice on the Conduct of Household Affairs in General; and Particular Directions for the Preservation of Furniture, Bedding, etc., For the Laying in and Preserving of Provisions; with a Complete Collection of Receipts for Economical Domestic Cookery, the Whole Carefully Prepared for The Use of American Housekeepers by a Lady."

The lady's advice sounds practical and sensible even now, a hundred and thirty years later. "A cook has many trials to her temper," she complains, "but none so difficult to bear as the annoyance of a bad [cooking] fire." We appreciate such a complaint on a night like this when we scrape with a sturdy thumbnail at the thick lace of frost on the Butt'ry window to watch the storm. Our winter thoughts are accustomed to worrying a bit about strong winds that blow heavy-laden branches from roadside trees across power lines, leaving country and town houses alike stranded without light or heat, sometimes for several days at a time. Well, our New England Boiled Dinner tonight was completed on a steadily glowing electric burner, but it could have been cooked over the coals of the hearthfire just as happily. And there is something very adventuresome and cozy about doing just that.

In the interest of American culinary history, I looked for receipts for New England Boiled Dinner in some of the old cookery books. Miss Maria Parloa, a favorite cookbook writer of the nineteenth century and a New Hampshire lady, gives excellent instructions for corning beef, but does not mention the Boiled Dinner as such in any of her cookbooks on my Butt'ry shelf.

Mrs. Mary Lincoln was head of the Boston Cooking School preceding Fannie Farmer. In her cookbook published in 1884, Mrs. Lincoln gives credit to "Mrs. Poor," whose identity is otherwise lost to us, for her Old-fashioned Boiled Dinner receipt. "Notwithstanding that this dish has fallen into ill-repute with many people [which perhaps accounts for Miss Parloa's having ignored it], it may be prepared so as to be both palatable and nutritious for those who exercise freely. It is more suitable for cold seasons," said Mrs. Lincoln.

In 1904, in a New England village church cookbook, a quotation was included in the receipt for Boiled Dinner: "Our old and faithful friend, we are glad to see you," a line from Shakespeare's *Measure for Measure*.

In spite of Mrs. Lincoln's admonition in 1884 that the dish was losing popularity, it is still made and enjoyed thoroughly in many a New England home today, nearly one hundred years later. It is often served at country church suppers. In a delightful red farmhouse we know well, Boiled Dinner is served on a cold winter's night to a busy and appreciative family, some of whom are willing to forsake their own hearths and drive quite a distance to partake of it.

New England Boiled Dinner is easy to prepare, and is a good hearty dinner for hungry people. It also contains about as much food value, vitamins, and flavor as one can get.

BUTT'RY BOOK BOILED DINNER

Wash 4 or 5 pounds of prime brisket of corned beef. Place the meat in a large kettle and cover with cold water. Cover the kettle and cook meat constantly at an easy simmer until almost tender, about an hour per pound of meat.

Then add vegetables: carrots, turnips, potatoes, an onion and parsnips, or vegetables to your taste which have been scrubbed and cut into convenient pieces for serving. Cover, and cook until the potatoes are nearly done (usually about 25 minutes). Then add a cabbage cut in eighths which has had its outer leaves trimmed and the core trimmed but not entirely removed. Cover and boil an additional 12 minutes.

Beets should be cooked separately, boiled until tender, then peeled and buttered.

Remove corned beef to a large hot platter, and surround with the vegetables, including beets. Put vinegar on the table if desired for Old-fashioned Boiled Dinner enthusiasts; or horseradish or mustard for those who prefer it.

Red Flannel Hash follows this dish the next day as day follows night or sunshine follows snowstorm.

RED FLANNEL HASH

Chop (do not grind) approximately equal parts of cabbage, beets, and turnips or parsnips, adding as much potato as there is of all the other vegetables—the leftovers from the Boiled Dinner. Chop and add the leftover corned beef and an onion. Mix all well together lightly. Add salt and pepper to taste.

Put a heaping tablespoonful of drippings or butter into a large frying pan. When hot, add the hash, cover lightly, and cook slowly until well heated through and browned on the bottom.

With this great dinner, a light refreshing dessert is home-made pineapple sherbet—there is no room for anything more.

PINEAPPLE SHERBET

1 can shredded pineapple (No. 2 can or 2 cups)	3½ cups sugar
2 cups pineapple juice	3 quarts whole milk
Juice of 4 lemons	1 pint heavy cream

BREAK THE COLD FROSTY SILENCE

Have all ingredients cold. Dissolve sugar in juices, add fruit and milk and stir all well together. It does not matter if the milk curdles a bit as the turning of the ice cream freezer smooths the mixture. Pour into freezer can, then stir in cream. Freeze, using one part ice cream salt to four parts of ice.

This receipt makes enough sherbet for a six-quart freezer.

Some hae meat and canna' eat,
  And some would eat that want it,
But we hae meat and we can eat,
  Sae let the Lord be thankit.

—ROBERT BURNS

Portrait—Wilson Alwyn Bentley

TREASURES OF THE SNOW

Hast thou entered into the treasures of the snow?
or hast thou seen the treasures of the hail . . . ?

—BOOK OF JOB

WHEN the first flakes of snow fall in an early winter storm, New Englanders welcome the sight and approve the full circle of nature's calendar of the seasons. All things need a time of rest, a change of pace, a fresh approach. Snow gives us this change; and it bestows upon the land a blanket which protects, enriches, and beautifies.

Of the countless trillions of snowflakes which fall in a storm, no two flakes have ever been found that are exactly alike. There are similarities, the most important one being that they are all based on a hexagonal pattern or variations of such a pattern. Some are flat six-sided little plates or plaques, some are six-pointed stars or flowers, some are like columns with six-sided plates at each end. Occasionally there are freaks caused by two or more flakes clinging together to make an unusual formation. Sometimes the sides or points are constricted to three or multiplied to twelve.

To examine a snowflake momentarily on a mitten before it melts and is gone forever is part of a child's curiosity about the world around him. To examine one through a little microscope was the experience of a young Vermont boy who became so fascinated with what he saw that he thereafter devoted his life to the study of the form, pattern, and origin of snowflakes.

Wilson Alwyn Bentley was born in a pleasant white house nestled in Mill Brook Valley in the shadow of Mount Mansfield near Jericho Center, Vermont, on February 9, 1865. His parents were good farmers and good people, old-fashioned, hard-working, not prosperous but in comfortable enough circumstances. There were two boys and a girl in the family who attended the district school whenever it opened intermittently for classes between stretches of bad weather. The rest of the time they were taught by their mother.

Wilson spent his summers in the usual Vermont boyhood pursuits: helping his father on the farm, fishing (he was a better than average hand at catching a fine trout), searching the fields for wild flowers, animal tracks, berries, and birds, and observing the storms which swept down the valley of the rushing Winooski River nearby.

The winters in his valley were intense and of long duration. To help fill his time, he mastered without a teacher a number of musical instruments including the piano, cornet, violin, and the large organ which stood in his mother's parlor, and he became adept at giving concerts in the local schoolhouse, always crowded for such an occasion. He composed much of his own music. He could imitate on his musical instruments all of the birdcalls he had heard in Mill Brook Valley, as well as the croaking of frogs, the barnyard voices and those of certain local characters of the town, and even the sound and fury of the thunderstorms.

He also loved to watch the snowstorms and to study the formation of frost and ice and snow. It was perhaps this interest that prompted his mother to buy for him as a birthday present a small crude microscope. The first thing he examined with it was a snowflake, and he was captivated for life, enchanted by its fragile beauty, its pattern, form, and structure.

The boy soon learned how to catch the flakes and transmit them to the glass plates of his microscope. With painstaking care he began drawing their intricate patterns as best he could, but it was a slow, difficult, and unsatisfactory way to make a record of them. With his mother's help and encouragement, he finally persuaded his reluctant father to buy for him a combination microscope and camera. Edwin Way Teale tells us that as long as he lived, Father Bentley considered this one-hundred-dollar expenditure to be an unnecessary extragavance for a farm boy who should have been more interested in milking cows and plowing fields than taking pictures of snowflakes. With ingenious pulleys, strings, and attachments of his own devising, Wilson used this same equipment for the rest of his life, taking over six thousand photographs of snowflakes, frost, dew, and raindrops.

At the door of a shed, cold as all outdoors, he would stand holding out a smooth black-painted or velvet-covered board. In order to prevent the transmission of heat or moisture from his mittened hands, he held the board with a wire handle. He would then examine all the flakes he had caught, brushing away damaged or uninteresting flakes with a tiny feather from a bird's wing. Just any snowflake would not do—it must be in perfect form. With a thin splinter of wood he touched the center of the flake which adhered to the wood just long enough to allow it to be transferred to the glass plate of the microscope. A gentle touch of the feather flattened the crystal so that he could examine and focus it. Since the light was at best dim in a snowstorm, he took time exposures. In this way he preserved forever the delicate crystal beauty of thousands of flakes.

His neighbors thought him a little crazy, chasing snowflakes in every storm. They called him "Snowflake" Bentley. His nature was so gentle, so quiet, so modest that they scarcely knew what he was accomplishing. He was only five feet four inches tall, slight, fair, with small dexterous hands and a serious but pleasant manner. After the death of his father, Wilson cared for his mother patiently and lovingly, never leaving her for more than a few hours at a time. He never married and shared the big white farmhouse with his brother and family, who continued to run the farm. He was amused rather than dismayed by the fact that his neighbors scoffed at him, but he was proud that he could see beauty in his surroundings which they were missing. During his lifetime, whenever Wilson made his way out into the world, he always hurried back to his homemade laboratory at the farm, eager never to miss a snowstorm, patient in recording its transitory beauty.

After a time Wilson Bentley was being asked to lecture in schools and colleges and to scientific groups all over the country. He contributed articles on snowflakes to the monthly *Weather Review* published by the U. S. Weather Bureau in Washington. He provided the photographs of dew, frost, snow, ice, and rain for a book by Jean M. Thompson called *Water Wonders Every Child Should Know* (New York: Doubleday, Page, 1913). He wrote for *Harper's Monthly*; and the *National Geographic* of January 1923, published his article "The Magic Beauty of Snow and Dew." He became a fellow of the American Meteorological Society and of the American Academy for the Advancement of Science. Men of scientific interest in weather, geography, and meteorology appreciated and learned from Wilson's studies, which he shared generously with them. Men with an interest in design eagerly sought his photographs from which they fashioned patterns for wallpaper, fabrics, glass, china, and jewelry. Tiffany's in New York bought some of his photographs from which were designed brooches and pendants for special customers. Interior decorators, art students, and housewives pored over his photographs for inspiration. Major colleges bought collections of his plates for their research libraries. Adaptations of designs from many of his photographs are still being used. In craft shops of New England sterling-silver snowflakes may be purchased in the form of pins, earrings, and pendants, even today.

Bentley was a self-educated scientist who constantly studied the phenomena of weather. At a glance, he could tell in what part of the sky a snowflake was wrought. He explained that the most perfect flakes came from the western segment of a low-pressure storm area, where the air was calmer and the flakes were less crowded as they fell. Storms which swept over a wide area of the country produced the even degrees of temperature and altitude in which the best flake characteristics developed and thus were the most suitable conditions for photographing.

The valley in which Wilson Bentley lived was the finest location possible in natural humidity and temperature for his microphotographs, and everything in nature around him in winter contributed something to his work —the windowpanes became deeply etched in frost, the trees were outlined in crystal splendors of ice design, and the snow crystals which fell onto his board were as perfectly formed as possible. Every great blizzard furnished him with new and beautiful crystals. That of March 12, 1888, was especially interesting in the opportunities it offered him. In the winter of 1900–1901 he found 133 new forms to photograph, the greatest number he ever recorded in one winter.

Bentley collaborated with a U. S. Weather Bureau scientist, W. J. Humphreys, to publish a book called *Snow Crystals* (available in reprint from Dover Publications, New York) which contains nearly 2,500 illustrations of his photographs. The photographs depict an infinite variety of exquisite designs, always in the three basic forms. Also included are some of his photographs of frost showing designs that resemble ferns, seaweed, curled feathers and scrolls, evergreen trees and moss, a peacock's tail, patterns of lace and embroidery, fringes and tassels. Dewdrops on spider webs might have been strings of crystal beads; and ice formations on grass, leaves, and flowers are jeweled wonders of nature.

Wilson Bentley at first believed he would someday find a duplicate of a snowflake design he had already discovered, but at length he decided no two could ever be alike, so different are the conditions which fashion their individual characteristics as they come swirling down from the sky. He was fascinated by this diversity, and his reaction to each flake was that of a scientist, as well as of an artist and even a poet, for his words in describing their beauty were poetic.

He died on a snowy day in December 1931, having been content to spend his whole lifetime in the white farmhouse on Mill Brook Road, with its smooth green lawn and old-fashioned cinnamon roses, and its ideal winter weather, surrounded by the Green Mountains.

On a pleasant day, we sought out the valley of the swift Winooski River and of the Mill Brook where Wilson Bentley had lived. The hills were snow-covered and placid. Neat Currier and Ives brick or clapboard houses with gingerbread trim and ruffled curtains dotted the country roads. We were within sight of Lake Champlain when we turned off the new highway onto the Jericho Road. Drifts of snow obscured the pastures; chickadees chattered in the evergreens. The old Bentley house is still standing, well preserved, pleasant, and gracious. In the front gable of the house, a painted snowflake pays tribute to the farm boy who had been born, lived, and died there. A fine lad greeted us as we stopped the car near the mailbox. "Do you have a lot of visitors?" we asked, to make conversation. "Yes, quite a few. Sometimes." It was a long way from the main roads, and there may not be many who know of the boy who loved snowflakes.

Driving away over the Green Mountains on Route 15, we entered the highlands where barns leaned from the wind, and many of their roofs had collapsed from the weight of heavy snows. A sign pointed the way to Smugglers Notch. We passed the Vermont Weatherboard Co., which advertises that it sells new wood with the authentic weathered-barn look. The snow was deep and the land was bleak in the winter afternoon.

Then the road rounded a hilltop from which we had a breathtaking view of the White Mountains of New Hampshire, their snowy peaks suddenly rosy in sunset. On these hills, on those peaks, snowflakes lost their identity, becoming one in the drifts and blankets across the mountaintops. This is the snow that children love, that skiers seek, that is of such concern to highway maintenance crews and driveway shovelers—the snow of the drifts and blankets. But to Wilson Alwyn Bentley, one flake at a time was worth a lifetime of devotion.

To him who in the love of Nature holds
Communion with her visible forms, she speaks
A various language. . . .
Go forth, under the open sky, and list
To Nature's teachings. . . .

—WILLIAM CULLEN BRYANT

FEBRUARY

Birthstone and Birthdays

February's Birthstone is the *Amethyst*, for *Sincerity*.

1	16
2	17
3	18
4	19
5	20
6	21
7	22
8	23
9	24
10	25
11	26
12	27
13	28
14	29
15	

Flower

THE AMARANTH
Amaranthus caudatus

THE old-fashioned name for this colorful plant was "Love Lies Bleeding," which may account for its choice as a flower for February, the month of Valentine's Day, in which plants denoting love had a special significance.

Amaranth has scarlet flowers and large colorful foliage. It is an annual, easily grown from seed, but for best effect should not be used too freely. The flowers and foliage are effective in flower arrangements.

It is said that the ancient gods wore wreaths of it; and Milton in his *Paradise Lost* crowns the angels with it. Its meaning to the ancients was Immortality or Unfading Love.

Amaranth prospers in the garden until frost.

———————————◆———————————

> Immortal Amaranth! a flower which once
> In paradise, fast by the tree of life
> Began to bloom; but soon, for man's offence,
> To heaven removed, where first it grew, there grows
> And flowers aloft, shading the tree of life.
> —MILTON, *Paradise Lost*

Bird

THE most optimistic and hopeful bird we know is the Song Sparrow, who arrives in the garden—if indeed he has ever left it—to sing his first Song of Spring in the wintry cold and dark of February. He starts his song sporadically, hesitatingly, as if he himself is a little doubtful that winter will ever go away. But he gains confidence and is in full voice by the end of February, singing his spirited and matchless melodies from the bushes near the birdfeeder.

His welcome song breaks the spell of winter. And it continues all summer, until in November there is a final hymn of Thanksgiving before a period of winter quiet. With sure instinct, the Song Sparrow broadcasts his cheerful February forecast with fully as much authority as any almanac or star or weatherman. He nearly always begins with three notes which sound like "Sweet, sweet, sweet. . . ." Thoreau wrote that the country girls hear in the sparrow's song "Maids, maids, maids, hang on your teakettle, teakettle-ettle-ettle," and this seems good advice on a day when the hearthfire is burning brightly and we are waiting for tea. As a child, I could hear "Tea, tea, tea, Polly put your teakettle on" in this song of the February bird.

The Song Sparrow is a member of the large sparrow family, of which there are over sixty species to be found in America, and our bird himself wanders widely, being found in every state on the mainland, even Alaska.

In New England, he may winter over in our brushy woodlands, without migrating southward if he has food and cover to his liking. His nest is built on or very near the ground, perphaps in the crotch of a shrub. The nest is of grass and leaves, lined with finer grass and hair. I have such a nest which I found one December, long deserted, and gathered it to put on the Christmas tree. The inner nest was intricately lined with horsehair, and as I knew of no horses within several miles, the transportation problems for building materials must have been quite formidable in this case. There are sometimes as many as three broods a year, and the eggs are bluish-white, spotted with brown.

The Song Sparrow is dainty of figure and size. His gray waistcoat is very gay with stripes of brown, and he carries a brown locket on his breast which is his sure identification. His tail is rather long and narrow, and it flicks as he darts about in the branches of his favorite haunts. He is happy and busy, tame enough to build nests in thickets near habitation, but darting quickly out of sight if danger threatens. He prefers living in thick shrubbery near houses, or in brushy places around abandoned fields or farms, and likes water nearby. His natural foods are insects and seeds which he finds on or near the ground. Occasionally in winter he will feed from the deck of the bird-feeder, but he really prefers gathering his meals from the provender which is scattered on the ground below.

Like an unexpected burst of sunshine on a stormy day, the song and presence of this bird cheers us immeasurably.

I sit and hear the blithe song-sparrow sing
His strain of rapture not to be suppressed . . .
That song of perfect trust, of perfect cheer,
Courageous, constant, free of doubt or fear.
—CELIA THAXTER

Break the Cold Frosty Silence

Come when the rains
Have glazed the snow and clothed the trees with ice,
While the slant sun of February pours
Into the bowers a flood of light.

—WILLIAM CULLEN BRYANT

THE long darkness of night is shrinking, and day is stretching after its winter rest, lasting now until the church bell tolls six o'clock. The longer daylight is one of the few signs of spring in New England, even as Arcturus gives us some hope late at night, creeping stealthily forward as if afraid to break the cold frosty silence of February's wintry expanse.

We linger at breakfast, watching the birds at the feeder. A pair of robins demolishes in minutes the cut halves of apples. How fat they are; how soft and brilliant their rusty feathers. No wonder, they've been well fed all winter on juniper berries, apples, plump raisins, and bits of ground beef.

Chickadees like to monopolize the sunflower seeds, but redpolls are not afraid to elbow their way to the table. Sparrows take what they want and on the ground the juncos love burrowing in the snow to find their share. A single mockingbird watches from the stark lilac for his turn at the raisins. And listen!—the first birdsong of the year—a song sparrow in the beach plum bushes. Happy sign, welcome sign.

A cardinal makes a smooth two-point landing on the lamppost and then swoops into the sunflower seeds, while chickadees and sparrows scold and chatter. We don't begrudge any of the sparrows their share of the feast, for we remember breakfasting under the apple tree one morning last summer and watching an English sparrow glean aphids from a rosebush, right down the stems as neatly as if he were eating corn on the cob. The birds in the garden are our friends.

The sky is darkened by depths of storm clouds, the snow becomes heavy. At last, we put on boots and arm ourselves with shovel and broom, then go into the garden to shovel a path to the mailbox and to shake heavy snow off the shrubs and trees. This we do with care, as too much energy can mean disaster in breaking brittle branches. If the fragile limbs seem lodged or frozen to the ground, we leave them to thaw in time. We are too late getting to the peach tree (grown from seeds we long ago tucked into the ground—"Don't waste a seed," we can hear Grandfather say): a great branch has torn away with a long gash and lies crushed in snow, leaving the tree with an espaliered look. When the sun comes out we will paint the gash with tree paint to protect it and to help it heal. A robin ducks into a little door he has found in the snow-laden juniper bush. So we leave him to his feasting on the silver berries, knowing the juniper has survived heavy storms for many winters without our help.

As the snow slackens we look for a break in the sky, for when the sun shines, these drifts will be as colorful as clouds, with ice-blue in the shadows, rosy-pink and lavender reflected from the sky.

It's Candlemas Day ("half the wood and half the hay") or Groundhog Day, take your choice of names. If the groundhog, or woodchuck, were foolish enough to come out of his den on this day, he would be discouraged, but who has ever really known one to venture forth in the winter just to predict the weather when he is so well equipped to sleep in his warm house until the clover and the grass are green?

The land is clean and pure and white, and the afternoon light wanes. *Tomorrow* will be great for skiing, dog sledding, snowshoeing, snowmobiling, great for a winter picnic!

Have you ever gone on a picnic in winter, a real picnic? It takes a picnic basket well filled with hearty sandwiches and plenty of hot soup and coffee. It takes plenty of warm clothes and good boots. Sometimes it takes also quite a lot of stamina to sit on a favorite rock on a lonely sea- and windswept beach, after a rugged walk along the shore. But the contrast between summer and winter in our familiar haunts is tremendous and beautiful.

We may find a snow-covered log at the edge of the river where we swim in summer, and watch the ice water tumble through its winter-heaped channels. Or drive to a mountaintop now teeming with skiers and join in the fun. Or follow the leader through the snow to a favorite pine tree in the woods, and find the tracks of deer and squirrels and weasels and rabbits. New England is full of winter picnic places, along the beaches, at the lakes, in the mountains, on the islands (weather permitting the ferryboat ride to get there), in one's own backyard. A picnic in the winter is exhilarating and exciting, to children and grown-ups alike—and how lovely to come home to the warmth and comfort of our own fireside. But this is for tomorrow.

The wind is gusty and strong. We make a stab at building a snowman, and with much piling and patting and shaping, Smoky the Bear becomes a great white hero of the garden, a polar bear in New England. Numb with cold, we turn back to the house with crunching footsteps. An armful of wood starts the hearthfire for drying mittens and warming people, and the kettle is filled for tea, delicious, steaming, heart- and toe-warming tea, which has refreshed New Englanders since about 1670 when it was introduced here.

The first license to sell tea was issued in 1690 to Messrs. Harris and Vernon in Boston. When tea first arrived in America, no one seemed to know just how to prepare or serve it. There was then no such thing in this country as a teapot, and it wasn't until unglazed stoneware teapots were brought from China with the tea that the proper vessel for making and serving it became available. It was but a short time until potters in Europe copied the designs and shapes of the Chinese ware; then silversmiths and pewterers, and porcelain manufacturers designed beautiful pots for serving the new beverage, which by the eighteenth century was becoming popular both in Europe and America.

It is said that when tea was first tried in this country, some amazing things were done with it. It was boiled; then the liquor was thrown away and the tea leaves eaten, sometimes with salt and butter, sometimes with sugar and milk. One delightful old book with illuminated pages describes the first Nantucket tea party where the hostess put a five-gallon bell-metal kettle of water on the crane, poured in four quarts of tea leaves and the whole was boiled for an hour, then the dark bitter liquor was drunk from silver porringers. Since this did not produce a very palatable beverage, the hostess entertained a practical suggestion that it had not been properly prepared and the liquor had best be used to dye woolen yarns.

Tea was first packed for shipment from Asia to America in jars and baskets, then in wooden chests lined with silver- or gold-coated papers known as "tea papers," or with sheet lead, to keep the processed tea dry and prevent its molding on the long ocean journey. In time, three principal kinds of tea were imported. Green tea was made from the unprocessed or unfermented dried leaves of the same shrub from which black, or fermented, tea was also obtained. A third kind, called oolong, was semifermented and tasted rather like a blend of the green and black. It is still the favorite of many ardent tea-drinkers. Now, approximately three hundred years after the first introduction of the beverage into America, we have many kinds and blends of tea, one of which, gunpowder tea, actually has the musty smoky fragrance and taste of gunpowder. Some of the modern blends include buds of fragrant flowers, orange peel, rose hips, spices, and herbs.

By the second half of the eighteenth century, tea-drinking had become a matter of social prestige in America. Although the beverage was esteemed also for its medicinal value in curing numerous fevers and aches, it was the social aspect that created its great popularity among prosperous American hostesses. Since both the tea and the tableware used in its preparation and serving were expensive, only the rich served the imported tea every day. It was kept under lock and key in boxes or "caddies" made for this purpose of wood, tortoise shell, silver, and porcelain. The hostess unlocked her box, spooned tea from the caddy into the pot with a small silver spoon, then locked the box again.

But on the sixteenth of December, 1773, there occurred that very famous tea party which was to affect not only the manners concerned with tea-drinking, but also the history of our country—the Boston Tea Party. From this time until after the Revolution, the drinking of real tea was scorned by the patriotic housewives of America. Instead, ladies held "Liberty Tea" parties, by means of which they protested the high tax on tea as well as many other wrongs with which they were oppressed by the Crown. From this protest action there grew the discovery by the great ladies of America (which those in less opulent circumstances had known all along) that delicious teas could be made from the herbs which grew in dooryard gardens and fields surrounding the towns and villages of all New England.

"Liberty Tea" was brewed from loosestrife leaves, which were processed rather like real tea, from dried wild strawberry and raspberry leaves, from rosemary and mint leaves, from catnip and sage and lemon verbena, from rose hips and many other delightfully tasty plants. The term came to mean any herb tea served to the Revolutionary dames in the spirit of their revolt. Every gossipy gathering of ladies (and often gentlemen) became a Liberty Tea Party. Very often a dainty little jug of rum was placed on the tea tray to enhance the flavor of the concoctions.

Today, as in the eighteenth century, tea-drinking can be a simple refreshing break in the day's activities, or it can be a gracious gesture of hospitality and sociability. Tea can be an excuse for having a party, or having a party can be an excuse for serving an elegant tea. We love tea by the fireside in winter, and in the garden in summer. We like to vary the kinds of tea. One trick is to put a rose geranium leaf or two into a pot of freshly made black tea. A sprig of lemon verbena or mint in the teacup is refreshing, too. For a change, we sometimes put a whole sprig of lemon balm, lemon verbena, or rosemary into the cup and pour boiling water over it—no milk, no sugar is needed; it is delightful in its own natural flavor.

There is no economy or joy in buying inexpensive teas, as they haven't good flavor to begin with, nor do they retain their flavor as long. Blending of fine teas is a highly developed art and so it is good to buy the very best quality available. A blend of fine teas such as will be found in many good food and specialty shops is in the long run more economical and certainly much more flavorful than cheaper brands.

Tea has little food value, but does contain very small quantities of vitamins, particularly if fresh herbs, or rose hips, or grated orange rind are added to it. Tea has qualities that refresh and relax, that warm and comfort. It was said in Victorian times that a good cup of tea would unlock all the secrets a woman carried in her heart.

The old rule of one teaspoon of tea for each cup and one for the pot is the best for fireside serving. The water must be fresh-drawn and freshly boiled. "Unless the teakettle boiling be, filling the teapot spoils the tea," a favorite rule of our grandmothers, is still good advice. The teapot must be preheated. Tea should be given three minutes to steep if it is to be drunk straight; or five minutes if milk or cream is to be added. Tea bags are convenient, but old-fashioned tea devotees have not yet succumbed to their convenience, saying that there is a difference in flavor. Porcelain or earthenware teapots hold the heat well and are the favorites of most tea-drinkers. Silver pots look elegant, and are often used for parties, although they do not retain heat as well as pottery, and sometimes a faint flavor of metal may be detected.

Today's tea trays always have the traditional lemon slices with cloves, a bowl of sugar cubes, and a pitcher of milk, but a change is delightful and welcome. The little jug of rum is a warming addition on a cold day—a touch does it. A tiny chunk of pineapple speared with a toothpick and put on the saucer is good to nibble. Add a bit of grated orange rind to the pot, and a few whole cloves. Add a sprig of mint or a rose geranium leaf; drop in a teaspoonful of good strained honey and stir it in well. Serve a pretty dish of candied orange or grapefruit peel, or crystallized flowers.* Candied ginger and tea go well together.

One of the most famous tea parties ever given was one which broke all the rules of propriety and nicety. Of course it wasn't held in America, it was in Wonderland, and the special guest was a young lady named Alice who hadn't even been invited. The hosts insulted each other and the guest, and the cups hadn't been washed or dried in ages. Worst of all, the party ended when one of the guests was ignominiously dunked in the teapot. Surely this is not the way to serve tea graciously, even in Wonderland. A simple and delectable choice of goodies to serve at tea will avoid such disastrous goings-on.

For tea sandwiches, we sometimes make rosemary butter. Spread thin slices of white bread with the butter, then cut with tiny cooky cutters into shapes.

* See my *New England Butt'ry Shelf Cookbook*, page 24.

ROSEMARY BUTTER

Cream well one-quarter pound of soft butter. Add to it one teaspoon of finely chopped fresh or dried rosemary. Cover and let stand in a cool (not cold, for ease in spreading) place for several hours before using.

MOTHER'S GINGER TEA CAKES

½ cup softened butter	1 tsp. salt
1 cup sugar	2 tsp. powdered ginger
2 eggs	1 tsp. cinnamon
⅔ cup dark molasses	1 tsp. powdered cloves
1 cup rich (whole) milk	1 tsp. baking soda
4 cups sifted flour	

Cream butter and sugar. Add eggs, molasses, and milk and stir well together. Mix all dry ingredients and stir into creamed mixture. Drop by half-teaspoons on greased cooky pans about an inch apart, and bake in preheated 400° oven for about 8 minutes (do not overbake).

When done, let stand a minute on cooky pans, then remove to cake racks to cool completely. Frost with an icing made of heavy cream and powdered sugar mixed to spreading consistency. When frosting has hardened, pack in a covered tin box with wax paper between layers of cookies.

QUAKER MAIDS

½ cup butter	1 tsp. baking powder
1 cup brown sugar	½ tsp. each salt, soda, nutmeg,
1 egg	powdered cloves
1 Tbs. vanilla	1 tsp. cinnamon
½ cup sour cream (or ⅓ cup	1 cup chopped nuts
milk)	1 cup chopped dates
1½ cups flour	1½ cups rolled oats

Cream together butter and sugar, then add egg, vanilla, and sour cream. Sift flour with other dry ingredients and add to creamed mixture. Fold in nuts, dates, and rolled oats. Drop by small or large teaspoonfuls depending on whether you want small (for tea) or large (for family) cookies, and bake on greased cooky sheets for 10 or 15 minutes at 375°, until delicately browned.

APRICOT-FILLED COOKIES

½ cup butter	2½ cups flour
1 cup sugar	2 tsp. baking powder
2 eggs, well beaten	1 tsp. lemon juice
1 Tbs. milk	Apricot jam

Cream butter and sugar and add eggs, milk, and lemon juice. Sift flour and baking powder and add to creamed mixture. Chill the dough for several hours. Divide dough in half, rolling out one-half at a time, on a floured board to about ⅛-inch thickness. Cut with a 2-inch round cooky or biscuit cutter. In the center of half of the rounds, put a small spoonful of jam. Cover the jam-filled cooky with a plain cooky. With a fork, press the edges of the two layers together all around the edges of each cooky. This will seal in the jam. Sprinkle the cookies lightly with sugar, and place on cooky sheet. Bake at 350° for about 15 minutes or until lightly browned. Remove from oven, let cool on sheet for 3 minutes, then remove with a spatula to a wire cake cooler. Other kinds of jam, or mincemeat, may be used with equal success.

DOUBLE CHOCOLATE TEA CAKES

3 squares bitter chocolate
1 6-oz. package chocolate-mint chips
2¼ cups sifted flour
¾ tsp. baking soda
½ tsp. salt
½ cup white sugar
½ cup firmly packed brown sugar
1 egg
⅔ cup soft butter
½ cup sour cream
1 Tbs. vanilla
1 cup chopped nuts

Melt the chocolate over boiling water; cool a little. Sift together flour, soda, and salt in a bowl. Add sugars, egg, butter, sour cream, vanilla all at once and mix well. Add melted chocolate and blend well. Add the chocolate-mint chips and chopped nuts and fold in well.

To make tea-size cookies, drop by half-teaspoonfuls 1 inch apart on ungreased cooky sheet. To make large cookies, drop by teaspoonfuls 2 inches apart. Bake at 375° for 10–12 minutes. This makes 150 tea cookies.

GILLIAN'S FRUIT TEA LOAF

1 cup hot tea
1 cup soft brown sugar
2 cups flour
1 Tbs. baking powder
1 cup black raisins
1 cup white raisins
1 cup chopped candied fruit
1 egg

In a bowl, combine fruits and sugar, and pour the hot tea over them. Allow to stand and soak for several hours. Add egg and mix well. Sift flour and baking powder into the mixture and stir until thoroughly blended. Preheat oven to 325°. Turn the batter into a greased 9-inch loaf pan and bake for about 1¼ hours, or until cake pulls away slightly from side of pan. Leave in pan 15 minutes, place on wire rack and cool.

This loaf is wonderfully easy to make. It contains no shortening but the fruit keeps it moist for several days. It is delicious sliced thin for tea, with or without butter; it is also useful for breakfast, lunch, or dinner, and is hearty for lunch-box sandwiches. It broiler-toasts well.

Portrait—Emily Dickinson

AN AMETHYST REMEMBRANCE

I held a jewel in my fingers
And went to sleep.
The day was warm, and winds were prosy;
I said: " 'Twill keep."

I woke and chid my honest fingers,—
The gem was gone;
And now an amethyst remembrance
Is all I own.

THE life and poetry of Emily Dickinson have always been surrounded by a mist of mystery and speculation. To a world which could not understand the delicate fabric of her genius, or the sensitive loneliness of her intellect, her actions were without reason. Why had she shut herself away from friends and the world? Had she been disappointed in love?—if not, how could she have written so many love poems? There are perhaps no better answers to these questions now than in the years immediately following the discovery of the poems she had left to a wondering world. But it may be that with the passage of years it is easier to understand her personality and genius.

She was born in Amherst, Massachusetts, in 1830 and she lived all her life of fifty-six years there in the large comfortable house her grandfather had built, surrounded by trees, flowers, hedges, and trellises. Her father was a highly respected citizen and lawyer, a pillar of the church, a stern, unbending Puritan who kept his family always under his supervision. He was said to have been generous with his worldly goods, if not of his spirit, and his family wanted nothing in the way of comfort.

Emily's mother was a plain, restrained, timid little woman and her married life was completely dominated by her husband.

As children, the three young Dickinsons lived the normal life of their time, the mid-nineteenth century. They were in better than comfortable circumstances and had a wide circle of friends. They went to church, enjoyed their naturally beautiful surroundings, lived quite simply. Emily attended for a time the South Hadley Female Seminary, which was founded primarily to educate possible mates for missionaries (it later became Mount Holyoke College), where her life seemed cramped and restrained away from the family circle. She later attended Amherst Academy. As a schoolgirl she was gay and witty, warm and natural. She enjoyed parties and was often the life of them. But as she grew up, she seemed more and more repressed, not seeming to find any close companion with whom she could share her thoughts.

Emily was plain, to be sure, but there is little in her writing to indicate that her plainness was much of a worry to her. She loved to dress in white and, as the years went by, wore no other color.

As a young woman she was friendly; from that time forward she withdrew more and more into seclusion until she was living in a world apart, sometimes even from her own family. She nevertheless continued to exhibit to those closest to her at home a thoughtfulness and generosity in giving and doing for them. But she did not share her mind, and eventually she did not set foot outside the grounds of her home. She seemingly had no wish or need for domesticity, or for fame, or for other companionship. She did not need to make a living. Her great need was to express herself and this she was doing in her seclusion, finding in her own heart and in her poetry all the companionship and outlet she needed.

The soul selects her own society,
Then shuts the door;
On her divine majority
Obtrude no more.

Emily loved words. She loved children and understood their magical imaginations and fantasies, and often made up poems for them which she sent to them tucked into little presents. She loved simplicity, and perhaps withdrew into seclusion because it was the simplest way of doing what she wanted to do: express her ideas and thoughts in poetry which no one whom she knew would understand. This was as natural to her as breathing, but the pretense of the people around her seemed unnatural.

Her most endearing poems, her brightest jewels, are those in which she portrays her love of nature, which she studied with pleasure and care—the song of a bird, the flight of a bee or a butterfly, the color of a petal; mushrooms, grass, spiders. Flowers were her constant delight. In her little conservatory she grew rare and beautiful flowers and it gave her happiness to share them with others, as she also occasionally shared bits of her poetry.

My nosegays are for Captives;
    Dim, long-expectant eyes,
Fingers denied the plucking,
    Patient till Paradise.

To such, if they should whisper
    Of morning and the moor,
They bear no other errand,
    And I, no other prayer.

She has often been characterized as a rare and strange spirit. Although her poetry depicts a certain individualism of thought, and her actions were not understood, her spirit was a soaring inquisitive thing—rare enough perhaps, but not strange for such a talented genius. Some of her poems on religion and eternity show the same kind of introspection which almost any of us has experienced at times. God to her was not the Puritan God in which her own father believed, but a personal mystery whose promises and nature she sought to understand. He was not necessarily found only in church, she thought, with a touch of her always delightful humor:

> Some keep the Sabbath going to church;
> I keep it staying at home,
> With a bobolink for a chorister,
> And an orchard for a dome.
>
> Some keep the Sabbath in surplice;
> I just wear my wings,
> And instead of tolling the bell for church,
> My little sexton sings.
>
> God preaches,—a noted clergyman,—
> And the sermon is never long;
> So instead of getting to heaven at last,
> I'm going all along!

Although she wrote more than six hundred poems, Emily Dickinson's family was not aware of it until after her death. Then her poems were discovered by her sister—forty-nine neat packets of them tied with slim thread. This was Emily's legacy to the world. After some of her poetry was published, critics complained that she was often oblivious to the rules of poetry —sometimes there is no rhyme, sometimes the meter is wrong; sometimes a word doesn't have any meaning; and the technique seems monotonous if one reads too many of the poems at one time.

But all these whimsicalities are part of the charm and special beauty of her verses. To prop a puzzling quatrain over the ironing board or kitchen table and read and think about it while doing the daily household chores makes the chores go quickly and the lines of the poem become clear and lovely. To read them is to understand her unique individuality and genius, and is to hold "an amethyst remembrance" of a rare and treasured gift.

This is my letter to the world,
That never wrote to me,—
The simple news that Nature told,
With tender majesty.

Her message is committed
To hands I cannot see;
For love of her, sweet countrymen,
Judge tenderly of me!

MARCH

Birthstone and Birthdays

The Birthstone for March is the *Bloodstone* or the *Aquamarine*, and the meaning for either gem is *Courage*.

1	16
2	17
3	18
4	19
5	20
6	21
7	22
8	23
9	24
10	25
11	26
12	27
13	28
14	29
15	30
	31

Flower

THE LARKSPUR
Delphinium

Larkspur lifting turquoise spires
Bluer than the sorcerer's fires.

THE Victorian interpretation for the Larkspur or Delphinium was lightness, fickleness, or haughtiness, which does not seem very appropriate to such a stately and reliable flower.

In old-fashioned gardens, the Larkspur (which was sometimes called Larks-heel) was always found, one of the few blue flowers there. It bloomed freely and luxuriantly all during the summer in all kinds of weather, and was generally left to seed itself for bloom the following year. It was a durable and satisfactory flower to enjoy in the garden or to cut for bouquets. We still call the annual variety of this plant the Larkspur, and we dignify the perennial variety by its botanical name, *Delphinium*. Both varieties have been highly improved over the years, with many new types and colors ranging from white and pink to deep purple.

The Larkspur and Delphinium are easy to grow, and do very well in rich soil, with a little coal or hardwood ashes dug into the soil around them. Seed of the Larkspur may be sown where the flower is to bloom, then thinned. Seed of the Delphinium is best planted in flats or cold frames in spring or early summer, then transplanted to the garden to bloom the second year.

Bird

THE AMERICAN ROBIN
Turgus migratorius

A voice went thro' the emerald land
And "Wake, wake, Robin," cried;
A brook burst out in laughter sweet,
And straight the winter sighed.

—ELLA HIGGINSON

THE American Robin is the bird of New England's state of Connecticut, and also of the states of Michigan and Wisconsin. He occupies a very special place in our affections, for he enjoys our company to the point where he will build a nest in our gardens, sometimes in a bush next to a door or window where he gives his concert, in rain or sunshine, knowing that he has appreciative listeners.

The Robin is a member of the thrush family. Unlike the shy thrushes of the woodlands, he is friendly and sociable. The first bird to waken in the morning, he is also the last to go to sleep at night, and his lullaby is one of the twilight's best features. Almost human in his expressions, a Robin in his calls and songs runs the gamut of emotions from good cheer and love, to anxiety and rage, and poignant sadness if he has lost his mate or his nest has been plundered.

His nest is loosely woven of straw and twigs, inside which he builds a plastered wall of mud and grass, and then he cushions the innermost part

of the nest with moss, soft grass, perhaps even a feather or two. The shape of
the nest is rounded out by a circular motion of the bird's feet and body.
Its three to five eggs are a delicate blue-green color which has given the
name to "robin's-egg blue."

Robins can have individual characteristics which make it easy to dis-
tinguish them from others of their family. For some years, we had a mother
Robin who was so possessive of the birdbath that she flew into a fury whenever any other approached it, scolding at the interlopers and plumping herself officiously into the middle of the bath for long periods of time. Another
Robin had an unusual warning call which alerted us to anything strange in
the yard—a neighbor coming through the gate to call, or a stray cat, dog,
woodchuck, or a new bird.

The young Robins exhibit in their spotted breasts one of the special
characteristics of the thrush family, and they seem to have the biggest mouths
in all the bird world when they are nestlings being fed.

More and more we see flocks of Robins staying over the winter in woods
and marshes of New England. They love the berries of juniper bushes and
mountain ash trees; relish pieces of apple; and fresh hamburger and plump
water-soaked raisins are to Robins as chocolate creams to us. In summer,
they eat and feed to their young untold quantities of cutworms, earthworms,
caterpillars, moths, and berries. Because they get up much earlier than we do,
they get a good many more pies from our cherry trees than we do—and we
are happy to share with them, considering it our ticket of admission for
many a summer evening's concert in the garden.

O Robin, robin, singing in the rain,
While black clouds lower
Above your bower!

—NORA PERRY

Poking in the Corners

The stormy March is come at last,
  With wind, and cloud, and changing skies;
I hear the rushing of the blast,
  That through the snowy valley flies.
                              —WILLIAM CULLEN BRYANT

MARCH is a play actor, an Indian giver. March is a warm soft spring day
and a sudden blizzard; a balmy breeze from the south and an icy blast from
the north; a sudden downpour and a blaze of bright sunshine. March is a
night sky of intense black and sparkling silver, or an awesome aurora bore-
alis of shimmering color, or a flash of lightning and a crash of thunder. But
the grandstanding doesn't fool us. The stars and planets have swung around
in place for the vernal equinox and the sun is warmer now than it was just
a few weeks ago.

Drifts of snow in the corners and along the stone walls and in the woods
are littered with broken twigs, the cones and needles of evergreens, the
acorn shells.

We watch the sky, straining eyes and ears to see the bobbing of the
first kite, to hear the first call of the bluebird, the song of a robin, the honk
of geese. Under the snow there are the buried seeds, the hidden roots, the
wakening buds. So much to look forward to! On banks of spring-flooded
brooks, the tightly folded blossoms and green leaves of skunk cabbage prick
their way through cold sodden leaf mold and give forth a strong odor in the
hope of persuading a sun-warmed fly to fertilize its blossom.

The earth is stirring, and by some subtle osmosis, spring is rising in the human heart, too. Country folks will be poking in the corners for signs—in a bare patch of ground under the shrubbery the white bells of the snowdrops and the yellow and blue tips of crocuses are showing color and will be open with a day of sun.

In the woods, a Christmas fern spreads last year's green and shining fronds. The sap is rising in the maples, and the buds are swelling on the birches. Squirrels will be searching the layers of last autumn's dead leaves to find a buried acorn. The farmer who today is providing well for his hearth by stacking the wood he has cut in the woodlots will be watching the temperatures for the warm days and freezing nights which mean a good sap run. On his way home he will take out his jackknife and cut some pussy willows for his wife to put into the old brown pot on the kitchen mantel.

We are hungry for spring. We paint the kitchen woodwork, paper the company room, plant the early seeds in flats. We go to town and buy a gay flowered dress and a pair of high-heeled patent leather slippers—or maybe just a new pair of sneakers. We fly a kite with a long string and a red and yellow tail.

A robin once more inspects the inviting but still bare branches of the crabapple tree next to the Butt'ry window, as he has for some years, in his eagerness to start building a new house there. But even as we watch him from the window, he whimpers, fluffs up his feathers in the cold wind, and we see with dismay that snow is falling. The flakes are big and soft and slowly swirling. Soon it blankets the garden.

So there is still time for the last of winter's tasks. We bring in the wood for the evening hearthfire, applewood is the favorite, with maple or oak for the backlog. The warmth of a hearthfire brings cheer and companionship to any household which has one.

No good New Englander could make a proper fire without a good bed of ashes. It keeps the wood from burning too fast; it reflects heat into the room instead of into the hearth bricks; it holds the heat in coals to make kindling fresh fuel easier. And when the fireplaces are cleaned out later in the spring, there is a valuable source of minerals in the ashes for irises and roses and lilacs and delphiniums. Our ancestors saved all the ashes for making lye and soap in a painstaking process which we are fortunate to be able to dispense with these days.

February and March are wood-gathering months for real country dwellers. The old saying is that wood we cut ourselves warms us twice—in the cutting and in the burning. There is a prosperous and thrifty look to the rows of cordwood piled between the maple trees down the lane, like a savings account in the bank. The wise farmer cuts only the dying or crippled or crowding trees, clearing his woodlot to let the good trees grow tall and straight. So our woodpile is a mixture of anything that needs thinning out— old butternut trees, which hiss and throw sparks as they burn in colors of gold and pink and purple and orange; ash and maple and oak which give slow-burning steady heat; old apple and cherry trees which in burning perfume the air with a pleasant incense, fragrant as bayberry candles; birch and beech which glow with a bright white flame; hickory which we like for broiling ham or steak or smoking sausage on the hearth. We love to watch the logs burn, some covered with gray lichen and colorful moss; some with plates of rough bark; some with smooth white papery curls.

We have heard of a country doctor who enjoyed cutting and stacking his own firewood. He inserted a clause in his will saying somewhat prophetically that he wanted to be buried in a chestnut coffin because chestnut crackled and snapped so cheerfully when it burned!

March in New England is town meeting time, and in the villages and towns in every state, the problems of local government are taken to the citizens, for better or for worse. Moderators of town meetings can have considerable power in shaping the affairs of their towns, for in some states they

are not bound by written rules of order, so can accept or reject many pro-
posals in clever ways to achieve political advantages. Town meeting can get
to be a pretty hot affair, and no one is ever really surprised when good friends
resort to name-calling and fist-waving and table-thumping. When the meeting is over, the combatants are usually as good friends as ever. We've known
cases, though, where families have come to a parting of the ways over town
meeting affairs.

Town meetings these days are being faced with something quite new
to the present generations of New Englanders—town planning. A lot of folks
say that no one is going to tell them what they can do with their land.
Their land was planned by their ancestors long ago. Old towns in New
England were well laid out originally, with a place for the meeting house,
the center of village life; with homes and shops and taverns located in certain places close around the village green. The towns were planned so that
no one was isolated away from his neighbors, for his own protection from
Indians, and fire, and weather. The towns were planned so that the first rude
dwellings, which were built simply, of necessity, would be replaced by substantial homes of sturdy materials. The houses were even planned architec-
turally to assume one of several popular forms. Stone walls were planned,
for boundaries and to keep a neighbor's cows and sheep where they belonged,
and to make good use of a plentiful commodity.

Town planning continued through the Federal period and into the industrial revolution in this country, when great mills were built along the
rivers that furnished abundant power for their operation. Some of the early
mill complexes of that period are now considered to be handsome architectural marvels of their time, unknown anywhere else in the world. But lack of
present intelligent planning is threatening these historical and architectural
landmarks.

Industrial developments then continued to be built so rapidly throughout New England that we began to lose sight of the value of good planning.

Mills and mill houses were often put up almost overnight of cheap materials in ugly styles which contributed to what later became slum areas of the cities. A very few years ago some farseeing people became aware that our New England towns and villages were losing their beauty and charm, and historic and real value. Some towns began taking steps to preserve these values; some were declared historic areas which could not henceforward be cluttered by unsuitable building; some established zoning laws to encourage better-planned areas for the sake of the children and adults who live in them, and for the generations to come.

So town meetings are hashing over these problems every March, and progress will be made by farseeing town fathers. Man's environmental problems have increased to the point where he himself is threatened. Our air must be safe from poisoning; our water from pollution; our flora and fauna from extinction; our towns, villages, and countryside from unscrupulous development. An ounce of prevention is still worth a pound of cure.

A question passed around in many of the groups gathered in the corners of Town Hall is, "How's the sap going to run this year?" We learned from the Indians how to gather sap and boil it down to make syrup, and though the equipment has been improved over the years, the methods are still about the same as they were when we first landed on these shores. Maple syrup is one of the indispensable products of her region to a New England housewife.

The syrup is the distilled essence of the maple tree, a thin, clear liquid which is boiled to a golden rich sweetness of incomparable flavor. It takes from thirty to fifty gallons of sap to boil down into one gallon of syrup, depending on weather and the quality of sap in various trees. It's an old custom in the large orchards to have a sugaring-off party, and in some areas such parties are now being given for profit, which helps to pay the taxes on the land. The warm syrup is poured onto snow, where it congeals and is

gathered into a candylike chewy piece. Tradition demands that fresh doughnuts and pickles (to counteract the sweetness of the syrup) are an important
part of such parties.

Many an intrepid novice is producing syrup successfully (although ex-
pensively, with today's high fuel costs) on the kitchen stove, after boring
several holes in the frontyard maples. Hollow "spiles" (spigots) can be hand-
whittled of pithy elderberry stems to push into the dripping holes in the
tree, or metal spiles may be bought in country hardware stores or farmers
exchanges. A notch carved into the top of the wooden spile will hold the
colorful plastic pails which are replacing the old handbound wooden buckets
of long ago. Poured into a roasting pan, or other large flat pan, the gathered
sap slowly simmers away in the kitchen of today's farmhouse as well as in
commercial orchard houses, as it has for three and a half centuries in New
England. The sap must be closely watched night and day so that it doesn't
burn or boil over. When the syrup reaches 220° on a candy thermometer,
it is ready to pour hot on the snow for "sugaring-off"; to put into jars and
seal; or to drench pancakes. What a triumph . . . how absolutely superior!

Throughout the year, maple syrup is on our table in its own cruet for
pouring over hot or cold cereal, hot corn bread, pancakes, and waffles. We
make muffins and fudge and maple mousse and maplenut ice cream; and
we pour the syrup over apples or a ham baking in the oven. We use it generously on French toast, and on vanilla ice cream, in sweet potato and squash
dishes. The *Butt'ry Shelf Cookbook* contains a receipt for maple graham
bread that is one of our standbys.

Maple mousse is an elegantly rich dish, fit for the best company occasions.

MAPLE MOUSSE

4 egg yolks
¾ cup pure maple syrup
1 pint heavy cream

In a double boiler, beat the egg yolks lightly. In a small pan, heat the maple syrup but do not boil; add very slowly to the beaten egg yolks, beating well. Cook over low fire or hot water until the mixture thickens, stirring constantly. Remove from fire.

With an egg beater or electric beater, beat the mixture until it becomes cool. Whip the cream until stiff. Fold the egg mixture very lightly into the whipped cream. Pour into a quart mold or ice cream can, then pack in four parts chopped ice to one part ice cream salt for at least 4 hours; or freeze in the coldest part of freezer for 4 hours. This does not require turning the freezer as in ice cream.

To serve, unmold on a pretty plate, garnish with chopped butternuts or black walnuts. Or spoon into individual glasses from the ice cream container.

FRENCH TOAST

In a low pan or dish large enough to hold flat 6 slices of bread, beat 3 eggs with a fork; add a dash of salt, 2 Tbs. sugar or maple syrup, ½ cup rich milk, and ¼ tsp. mace, and beat all lightly together. Put 6 slices of 2- or 3-day-old bread into this mixture, let stand a few minutes, then turn slices over. This may be prepared the night before and left covered overnight in the refrigerator to absorb all the batter if desired.

When ready to prepare, heat a flat griddle fairly hot as for pancakes, and melt on it 3 Tbs. butter until it bubbles gently. Fry the slices quickly until brown on one side, turn with pancake turner and brown well on the other side. Serve hot, dust with powdered sugar if desired, accompanied by a pitcherful of maple syrup.

MAPLE BUTTERNUT CREAMS

1½ cup white sugar
½ cup maple sugar
⅔ cup heavy sweet cream or commercial sour cream
2 Tbs. milk

Pinch of salt
¼ tsp. almond extract
½ cup chopped butternuts (or black walnuts)
1 Tbs. butter

Mix sugars, cream, milk, and salt together in generous-size saucepan. To avoid having the candy crystallize, butter a rim around the inside of saucepan above ingredients. Stir mixture thoroughly and heat to boiling point, still stirring until all sugar is dissolved. When mixture starts to boil, turn heat down somewhat and cease stirring. Begin testing after 3 minutes of cooking. Remove from fire at soft ball stage (or 238° on a candy thermometer). Add butter but do not stir. Cool until lukewarm. Add almond flavoring and stir candy until smooth and creamy, just holding shape. Add nuts, form into bonbons with teaspoon, and place drops on buttered cooky sheet. Or pour the whole mixture into a buttered pan and cut into squares when cold. Makes about 50 pieces.

MAPLE CUSTARD

In a bowl beat together:

4 medium eggs   ½ cup maple syrup

Slowly stir this mixture into 1¾ cups scalded milk to which a pinch of salt has been added. Pour into 6 large custard cups which have been placed in a pan of hot water. Bake at 325° for 35–45 minutes or until paring knife inserted in center comes out clean. May be served warm or chilled. Chopped nuts may be served on top as garnish.

Custard which cooks too long or at too high a temperature may separate.

A little house well fill'd, a little field well till'd,
and a little wife well will'd, are great riches.

—POOR RICHARD

Portrait—The Smith Sisters

VICTORY IN GLASTONBURY

A HUNDRED YEARS ago there lived in Glastonbury, Connecticut, two gentle elderly spinsters who might have stepped directly from the pages of Mrs. Gaskell's once popular novel *Cranford*, complete with Alderney cows.

These ladies were the last of five sisters who had been born and raised in a big farmhouse on the banks of the Connecticut River, daughters of Zephaniah Hollister Smith, a minister, lawyer, and farmer, and Hannah Hadassah Smith, one of whose accomplishments was a knowledge of astronomy, another the compilation of an almanac for her own use and that of her neighbors. The five sisters had an impressive background of parent-administered education, for they spoke many languages and read many volumes. One of the sisters translated the complete Bible into English from Latin, from Greek, and from Hebrew. They also had unusual names: Hancy Zephina, Cyrinthia Sacretia, Laurilla Aleroyla, Julia Evelina, and Abby Hadassah. The two gentle ladies who concern us here are Julia and Abby.

In addition to their zeal for learning, the two sisters ran their farm, which was well located in the fertile river valley. They milked their pet Alderney cows and made cheese and butter. They spun wool from their sheep and wove cloth from the yarn thereof. They filled their leisure hours with good deeds among their neighbors, the poor and the sick. And they watched with interest the progress of their contemporaries who were fighting the battles of women's suffrage, as in earlier days they had participated with enthusiasm in the antislavery movement.

By 1873 the two sisters, the last of their family, were content to devote their days to the tasks of their home. But it was not to be so. For in that year, the Glastonbury tax collector announced to the ladies (who were already the town's leading taxpayers) that their land had been reassessed and the tax raised. Two other ladies in the town, widows, were given a like notice. Curiously enough, however, the Smith sisters found that property of none of the men in town had been so assessed. The ladies were justly and righteously incensed that they—who could not even vote nor have any voice whatever in how their tax money was spent—should be so discriminated against. It was surely a case of "taxation without representation," and their consciences moved them to do something about it.

The two sisters appeared at the next town meeting—a gathering unaccustomed to the presence of women—and the moderator reluctantly gave Abby an opportunity to speak her piece. It fell on deaf ears, and the meeting then went on as if the ladies were not present, in spite of the eloquence of Abby's presentation. And so the sisters decided that their only course was a refusal to pay the unjust tax, even though they realized it could mean trouble for them.

And trouble they found. There were at that time considerable amounts in back taxes owed to the town by other property owners and no effort was made to collect these except for interest. But in the case of the Smith sisters, the tax collector shortly hied himself to their farm and attached seven of their beloved Alderney cows—of considerable worth—to satisfy the $101.39 which the ladies now owed in taxes. When the cows were placed at auction, the sisters asked a friend to bid them in, and the cows were returned to their own stalls.

These events simply strengthened their resolution to fight for their stand. "Taxation without representation," echoing an earlier battle cry, again became a famous slogan, this time by sympathizing women suffragettes all over the country who were urging rights for women.

The following year, when their taxes became due, the Smith sisters again appeared at town meeting to plead their case. But the moderator refused to grant their petition to speak. This time the tax collector advertised a part of their farm to be sold at public auction, and land worth several thousand dollars was sold for $78.35 in taxes. Since the sisters were unable to locate the place of sale (which was adroitly kept secret from all except a privileged few), they were prevented from buying back what rightly was theirs.

Now Abby and Julia switched their course a bit and decided to sue the tax collector, for though he was legally entitled to attach personal property in payment of taxes, seizing their land was unlawful. The first case was decided in their favor, but the tax collector appealed. The second case was decided against them, and under very strange circumstances, so the sisters appealed.

Interest in the case was countrywide, and the Smith sisters were now famous. Samuel Bowles, well-known and respected editor of the Springfield, Massachusetts, *Republican*, established a fund for them and contributions poured in. Newspaper reporters from everywhere came to Glastonbury to enjoy the hospitality of the charming elderly sisters, and to get material for stories. Julia decided to publish her translation of the Bible, for the monetary aid and publicity value to their cause. Abby wrote letters and articles for publication, and great must have been the chagrin of the Glastonbury tax collector and town fathers to see what their discrimination against two "helpless" ladies in their eighties had wrought. No one enjoyed the whole affair more than the sisters themselves, who had known all along that they were in the right.

The Smith sisters won their case finally, much to the joy of suffragettes everywhere. Julia and Abby accepted their victory with quiet humor and dignity, being mindful that they were fortunate to have sacrificed only property and time to the cause, while "our forefathers gave up their lives" fighting for the same principles. Abby wrote a little volume called *Abby*

Smith and Her Cows which tells the delightful story. The book is now a much-sought-after collector's item.

In a few years, Abby, who was the apparent leader of the two, parted from this life and from the burden of taxes, leaving her elder sister Julia lonely and aging. A cousin from Vermont was persuaded to help her with the care of the farm, on the understanding that he would inherit her property. But when an admirer of her accomplishments proposed marriage to her, she finally accepted, perhaps with some misgivings. Before long her new husband, retired Judge Amos A. Parker, issued an order that the Connecticut River farm and its contents be sold at auction, which left the cousin stranded and Miss Julia without her old home and possessions. As a married woman of that time, Julia had no legal right to dispute her husband's order to dispose of her property. What a difficult time it must have been for a woman nearing ninety—to marry, to give up her home and treasures, to move away to Fitzwilliam, New Hampshire, and to change her life completely. But she no longer had the counsel of her sister Abby and some burdens must have been heavy for her to bear.

Her last years were not happy ones, but she had her memories. When she died at ninety-four, she was buried in her own family cemetery with the other Smith sisters, the gravestone marked with her maiden name at her own request.

Nowadays, there is a difference of opinion, mostly among men, as to the effect for the better of women's participation in politics, although we no longer give any thought to their right to it. Town meetings are sometimes marked by women's voices, be they calm or discordant, raised in defense of their views. But two things are certain: the Smith sisters and their Alderney cows gave considerable impetus to the cause which eventually resulted in the passage of the Nineteenth Amendment to our Constitution; and they kept things lively during their lifetime in Glastonbury, Connecticut.

Dear March, come in!
How glad I am!
I looked for you before.
Put down your hat—
You must have walked—
How out of breath you are!
Dear March, how are you?

—EMILY DICKINSON

APRIL

Birthstone and Birthdays

April's Birthstone is the *Diamond*, meaning *Innocence*.

1	16
2	17
3	18
4	19
5	20
6	21
7	22
8	23
9	24
10	25
11	26
12	27
13	28
14	29
15	30

Flower

THE MOUNTAIN LAUREL
Kalmia latifolia

AMONG interpretations of the meaning of flowers, the Mountain Laurel sometimes had a connotation of Ambition. Other earlier meanings suggested Glory, for which Laurel wreaths were given; and Sarah Josepha Hale in *Flora's Interpreter* suggested a meaning of Virtue.

The Mountain Laurel is a native of eastern North America, where it brightens woods from the Carolinas north to Canada, and it is the state flower of Connecticut. Its season of bloom in New England is late May and June. The delicate white star-shaped flowers are marked with pink or lavender in such a way as to have given it the familiar name of "calico bush" by which it is known to most country people. Its botanical name was given to it in honor of Peter Kalm, the Swedish botanist who came to America in the eighteenth century to study native plants.

Leaves of the Mountain Laurel are long and narrow and evergreen. At Christmas time swags of the branches entwine doorways and lampposts, and festoon mantels and stairways. The leaves are used year round for background material for flower arrangements.

Mountain Laurel makes a very handsome shrub for home gardens, preferring an acid soil, as do other members of the heath family of plants. In suitable conditions, individual bushes become as tall as small trees. In spring, it is worth going many miles to see the woods of Laurel in bloom.

Shakespeare was not accounted great
When good Queen Bess ruled England's state,
So why should I today repine
Because the laurel is not mine?

                      —JOHN K. BANGS

Bird

THE EASTERN BLUEBIRD
Sialia sialis

Rise up, my love, my fair one, and come away. For,
lo, the winter is past, the rain is over and gone; the
flowers appear upon the earth; the time of the singing
of the birds is come. . . .

—THE SONG OF SOLOMON

THERE comes a dawning in early spring when a faint, sweet plaintive call from the garden tells us unmistakably, not that spring is on its way, but that spring is here. It is the Bluebird come to announce his arrival and say that all is well. His gentle "Dee-ar me" on a rising note is the most welcome sound to me of springtime, for the Bluebird is my own favorite bird, symbol of all that is good—beauty, honesty, courage, pride, love of home and family. The Bluebird is said to carry the blue of the sky on his back, the red earth on his breast, the purity of clean snow under his tail—our national colors.

There have been springs when his soft delicate warbling was not heard in the garden, and something very important to the season was sorely missed. The Bluebird has suffered immeasurably from man's insect and weed spraying programs and from man and nature through the introduction of the starling and English sparrow to this country; birds which have usurped many of his nesting places. Only the most urgent community devotion to nesting projects can save the Bluebird from extinction.

In the spring, the male usually appears in the garden first, perching on the butternut tree at the head of the lane, where he has a good view of the garden. He announces his arrival, then flies away, and we see him return in a few days with his wife. Together they chat and talk softly together in the trees, around the barn and henhouse, discussing the future, and considering all possible building places. They have a wide variety of possibilities —old apple trees full of fine holes; a dozen or so houses nailed to trees and fenceposts down the lane and in the orchard; even a house just their size nailed to the corner of our own house under the window where we can hear them as they greet the dawn each morning.

The Bluebirds' soft coaxing lovenote is one of the most touching sounds of nature. When danger threatens, they rasp out a distinct sputtering scold and snap their bills with vigor. When the young are ready to come out of the nest, the parents sit on the branch of a nearby tree and coax softly until, one at a time, the nestlings fly to them. It is amazing to see with what strength the young fly for the first time—they go straight to a perch with no hesitation and no need to rely on the ground for a landing spot.

After the first brood, the parents take the youngsters down the lane and into the woods, to teach them to find their own food. In a week or so, the parents return and rebuild their nest (we clean out their boxes for them as soon as the first family is gone) for another brood. The first young continue to hover nearby and in fact all summer the whole family enjoys being together, gathering at bath time and treating themselves to cutworms and beetles from the garden in a gay picnic until at last they head south together in the late fall.

Our Bluebirds perch on a corner of the house, or on the open branch of the butternut tree searching for bugs. They swoop down to snap up their prey, then back to the perch, balancing with a flick of their tails. We watch with amusement as the parents take the young to the birdbath for the first time—parents in the water splashing and spluttering; babies perched on the rim going through the same antics in the shower of water from the parents. Soon they are all in it together and, with a great deal of animated conversation, have one great family swim.

We have seen the devotion of the Bluebirds to each other manifested over and over again, a particularly warm affectionate loyalty. One early morning, our neighbor's adored cat Pansy succeeded in catching a mother Bluebird who in her anxiety to find food for her newly hatched family was not watchful enough. For two days the father continued a haphazard feeding of the babies interspersed with a sad, lonely call for his mate which was heartbreaking to hear. Then he seemed to gather himself together. With constant diligence he fed the four young in the nest, never ceasing during the daylight hours, making trip after trip after trip to the mouths of those hungry little birds, until they were ready to fly. At the end of the period, the father bird was thin, scrawny, and colorless. We didn't see him for two or three weeks, then he returned to the garden to recuperate for the long trip south, and by autumn was himself again—still without a mate, but with the young birds hovering around him.

Bluebirds are members of the large thrush family, and the young, like young robins, carry the family escutcheon on their breasts in dark spots which they soon lose. Their loose nest is made of grass and small sticks and is not very tidily built, although it is kept quite clean by the parents. There are usually four pretty, light-blue eggs. They eat quantities of cutworms, moths, beetles, and caterpillars, and are of especial value in the garden and orchard.

Houses built for them should be placed at least a hundred feet apart for good bird-community relations, on fenceposts, outbuildings, or trees, and are best left unpainted. The Audubon Society has been diligent in encouraging nesting sites for these beautiful birds, and will send on request leaflets giving complete instructions for attracting them and for building Bluebird houses.

In the budding woods the April days,
Faint with fragrance from the life begun,
Where the early fluttering sunbeam plays
Like a prisoned creature of the sun,
With sweet trill or plaintive note,
Quick pulsation of a throat,
With the life and light of Spring
There the birds of April sing.

—DORA READ GOODALE

Gather a Basketful

"Sing a song of Spring," cried the pleasant April rain
With a thousand sparkling tones upon the window pane,
And the flowers hidden in the ground woke dreamily and
    stirred,
From root to root, from seed to seed, crept swiftly the
    happy word.

                                            —CELIA THAXTER

GREEN FOLIAGE of spring hurries to cover the scars of winter. The earth warms. In ponds and swamps spring peepers tune up their sleigh-bell chorus in a wave of song. Meadows are golden with marsh marigold and we put on our boots to gather a basketful for floating in an amber dish. We find every excuse to be out-of-doors and even the threat of spring housecleaning does not deter us.

Twigs and leaves and last autumn's debris are raked from the garden, lawns are seeded and encouraged to greening for the summer. We turn the compost and revel in the rich humus ready for spring potting and planting. In observance of Arbor Day, we plant fruit and shade trees while they are dormant, digging plenty of compost and bone meal into the soil and firming it well around the roots of the newly planted trees. April is an ambitious month, plans for gardening burgeon expansively with little thought of the laziness of summer to come.

According to the plan we made in January, we outline the "wheel" for the herb garden. Turf is dug, stacked upside down against the stone wall and planted with thyme to make a garden seat akin to the "wattle seat" of eighteenth-century gardens. Inside the wheel we mix sand and leaf mold with the earth, and put the bricks in place for outlining wheel and spokes.

Bluebirds are calling from the trees in the lane, and have taken possession of their headquarters. An oriole shouts from the top of the elm tree; a phoebe pokes into the open henhouse window. Green fingers of daffodils swell into blossom and nod gently in rain or sunshine. An early tulip braves the spring chill and we agree with it that April is pleasant—but May will be even better. If we contemplate too much activity in the garden, a meadow-lark will remind us that "It's early." For in April spring moves deliberately, it has so much to do before May arrives.

Waving flags of the season, golden tassels of birch and maple combine with swelling purple buds of oak and beech to liven the color against spring skies. On the floor of the woods, shy wild flowers begin to appear on slopes splashed by warming sun—the pale anemone, the rare arbutus, a dusky blossom of wild ginger, a snowy bloodroot unrolling its delicate petals. In warm damp corners, the tight fiddleheads thrust through mats of dead leaves toward the sunlight. The brook sings in harmony with birds. The woodchuck stretches and ventures into the sunlight hungry for his first good meal of the year. Spring fever takes hold of man and beast and bird and flower in a delightful surge of activity.

But April rain can put a damper on enthusiasm. It falls gently, soaking down to roots; or it pours in torrents running off into the brooks with the very last of the melting snow.

> April weeps—but O ye hours!
> Follow with May's fairest flowers.
> —PERCY BYSSHE SHELLEY

The wind turns cold, daffodils huddle in the grass, and birds fluff their feathers for warmth on a sheltered branch. We love the sound of rain on the roof, a musical, rhythmic, soothing sound that would lull us into napping if we would let it.

The fish runs are one of the inimitable signs of New England spring-time. They are one of the constant and mysterious wonders of nature. When the alewives, which are sometimes called "buckies," or "whops," are running (why do we say "run," when obviously what they do is swim?) we grab our net and head for the little brook below the Gilbert Stuart birthplace in southern Rhode Island.

This mysterious migration of the alewives has been going on forever, and will go on in the future if we put no further obstacles in the way. Thanks to modern civilization, however, the spring fish runs of New England have dwindled and in many places have ceased altogether.

The Old Snuff Mill which was built by Gilbert Stuart's father has seen the running of the buckies for over two hundred years. As a boy, Gilbert could stand on the banks of this, his father's own brook, and catch all the fish he wanted. Undoubtedly his father salted away a good many for winter use. The quiet pool at the head of the brook is still serene, pure, and unpolluted just as it was in Gilbert Stuart's day.

Alewives are cousins of the herring. They swim from the Atlantic up the coastal streams heading for their spawning grounds in some inland pond or lake, and move in a mass at times so thick that they can be caught easily, even with the hands. At first it is hard to see them in the dark rippling waters of the brook, until a fin flashes out of the water in the sunlight and we realize that they fill the stream. We can often smell them, too, as boys from the neighborhood catch them recklessly and throw away the ones they don't want, so that the banks and waters of the stream are sometimes littered with gleaming scales and dead fish.

On a good day, when the sun is shining warmly and the birds are singing in the thickets above the little brook, we take off our sneakers and step into numbing cold water to shove out the net and pull in a good catch. The fish are bony, but quite delicious to eat when coated with crumbs or meal and fried in butter. The reddish roe of the female is delicately flavored when sautéed in butter, but the white milt found in the male alewives is not for eating.

Our forefathers learned from the Indians how to catch these plentiful fish and use them for fertilizer in their fields. One fish in one hill of corn guaranteed a good yield, three were better. It is not particularly pleasant to imagine the fragrance of a fine spring day as a soft wind blew across a field being so fertilized, but it kept our ancestors from being hungry at harvest time. The fish are said to have been gathered by wagonloads and peddled to farmers for fertilizer, or were salted and smoked and sold to housewives in the towns and villages across the countryside.

In days gone by, the salmon and shad runs were equally as tremendous. But our penchant for building dams and spreading pollution has put an end to most spawning runs for many years now. Millions of dollars are being spent these days in an attempt to undo some of our own damage. The salmon have suffered most from our depredations, having been literally obliterated from New England streams. The shad, however, have miraculously survived, although in much diminished numbers. There are still a few rivers where a lively shad can be caught with rod and reel to enrich a springtime dinner table with fish and a breakfast or luncheon omelet with roe. The Connecticut River and the Palmer River, for instance, are watched with keen anticipation by the sporting fishermen for the first April signs of shad. The flies are all tied, the spinners and spoons (take your choice of lure) polished and ready when the shad begin their upstream journey headed for the spawning grounds of their ancestors.

Few of these New England shad reach the fish markets, but those from the waters of mid-Atlantic states are found here in markets in season, together with the roe so highly prized by epicures. We like to buy a whole roe-shad weighing from four to six pounds (although some devotees believe the buck-shad has a richer flavor) because of the extra dividend of the high-priced roe. We ask the butcher to clean the fish, have the scales and head removed. We long-bake it whole to tenderness and rich succulence so that bones are dissolved in the baking. There is no better springtime treat than this delicious fish, and we relish the roe in a golden omelet.

Shad was once upon a time cooked on a board. It was cleaned, split, and butterflied, then nailed to a board which was propped before the hearth-fire, with salt pork stuck on the tops of the nails. For cookouts, this is still sometimes done, but because of the scarcity of the fish, it is almost a way of the past.

Early New England fishermen used to stretch a long net across the streams to catch the fish at spawning time. They did most of their fishing at night, and their catches were always generous. Sometimes the fish were so thick in the streams that they jammed, making it easy to harvest them in quantity.

In those days, many of the shad—like other fish—were smoked. They were so plentiful that they, too, were plowed into the fields as fertilizer, and sometimes were harvested just for the roe, the rest of the fish being thrown away. The roe was often used only for bass bait, which is interesting in view of the current extravagantly high price of roe.

The first arrival of shad used to be chalked up on the boards at fish markets and it was a real sign of spring. Since the runs in many areas coincided with the blossoming of the amelanchier, that delightful native shrub or tree was called a "shadbush" by early New Englanders, and it is so called to this day. When in bloom, the shad-blow is a drift of feathery white in the borders of New England woods. Birds love to eat the small red fruits which it bears. The tree transplants easily from the woods or nursery and is a most satisfactory small tree to have in a garden. We shall plant one for Arbor Day.

What does he plant who plants a tree?
He plants the friend of sun and sky;
He plants the flag of breezes free;
The shaft of beauty towering high.

—HENRY CUYLER BUNNER

SHAD ROE OMELET

One ought to be fussy about the pan used for omelets. It should be wiped clean with paper towels after use; water should be used only if the omelet has stuck to the pan, and soap should never be used or the fine coating of waxy oil will lose its effectiveness. A pan used for omelets should not be used for anything else. To prepare a frying pan with sloping sides for use in making omelets, rub it with a fine steel wool pad until it is as smooth as glass. Pour several tablespoons of olive oil into it, and put on very low heat for at least an hour, rubbing the olive oil around inside the pan occasionally with paper towels. Cool the pan and wipe with paper towels until smooth and clean.

For the omelet, use two frying pans: an omelet pan, and another small pan in which the shad roe can be sautéed. Sauté the roe quickly in a tablespoon of butter until browned, sprinkle juice of a quarter of lemon over it, and keep warm until omelet is ready.

6 eggs	fresh-ground pepper to taste
6 Tbs. rich milk or cream	1 generous Tbs. butter
pinch of salt	

Heat the omelet pan until the pan is hot enough to sputter drops of water flicked onto it. Put in the butter and melt it, then swirl butter around to cover bottom and sides of pan.

Beat eggs until light and fluffy. Beat in the milk (or cream) and the salt; add ground pepper to your taste.

Pour eggs into pan on a low fire, and let stand for a moment until eggs begin to set. As omelet sets around the sides, with a narrow spatula lift the sides of the omelet and tilt the pan to allow the uncooked eggs to flow underneath. Soon all the uncooked portion will have mixed with the cooked and eggs will seem set. Do not cook too long or at too high a heat. If omelet is overcooked it will be dry and tasteless. Allow center portion to remain shiny and light though not liquid.

Place browned roe on one side of the omelet, fold half of omelet over it with the spatula, and tilting the pan roll omelet onto a hot serving platter. Garnish with parsley or chervil. This serves four.

BAKED BONELESS SHAD

Have the fishmonger scale and clean a roe-shad, being careful not to cut into the roe. Save the roe to use with omelet for luncheon or breakfast.

Season the shad well with salt and pepper, then stuff with herb dressing; truss with pins and string. Put into a buttered baking dish which is long enough to hold the entire fish, and dust fish with paprika, sprinkle with lemon juice, and dot thoroughly with butter. Pour a cup of good dry white wine into the dish.

Wrap dish and all in heavy aluminum foil, make a "drugstore fold" (double fold) across the center, fold ends of foil securely. Put the dish into a preheated 450° oven for 10 minutes; reduce heat to 275° and cook slowly for 5 hours.

Remove foil for serving, garnish baking dish and fish with parsley and lemon wedges. This long slow cooking makes the bones soft and the fish will be rich and delicious.

ALEWIFE ROE FOR COCKTAIL SPREAD

In a generous tablespoon of butter, sauté the roe of female alewives, mashing with a fork as it cooks. Cook about 5 minutes or until all the roe has been lightly browned. Remove from fire, sprinkle with lemon juice. Mix enough mayonnaise with the mashed roe to make it of easy spreading consistency.

EVERY LEAF A MIRACLE

Portrait—Gilbert Stuart

AN EMPTY PURSE

ONE fine summer's afternoon some years ago, between concerts at the Berkshire Music Festival in western Massachusetts, we chanced into a little roadside junkshop without having much hope of finding a treasure. Just as we turned to leave, one of us caught the glint of gold leaf on an old picture frame stuffed behind other things, and we hauled into the light a framed engraving of George Washington. The glass was so coated with dirt that we could not see the details of the picture, but we liked the frame, which in spite of its grime was in quite good condition.

"I'll be glad to get rid of that thing," the junkman said, "and if you'll exchange it for another engraving of Washington—on a dollar bill—it's yours." We walked away with the picture, feeling that it was a good enough bargain.

Some time later, we began spending some part of each year near Saunderstown, Rhode Island, where on December 3, 1755, the great artist Gilbert Stuart was born, known especially for his fine portraits of George Washington. Looking for pictures to hang on the wall of our cottage there, we thought it time that the neglected gold-leaf-framed engraving of Mr. Washington be unearthed from its storage place in the barn, and brought it out for a cleaning.

The engraving was in good condition, though slightly water-marked and a little darkened from age, but the inscription under the picture suddenly became of much interest.

Painted by Gilbert Stuart 1797
Engraved by James Heath, Historical Engraver to His
Majesty and to His Royal Highness the Prince of Wales.
From the original picture in the collection of the
Marquis of Lansdowne

The original painting of this view of Washington was commissioned of Gilbert Stuart by the Marquis of Lansdowne of England, and it was painted while the artist resided in Philadelphia. When completed, it created an immediate sensation. In England a crafty engraver named James Heath, whom Stuart had known when he lived in England, soon perceived the financial advantage which would be his in making engraved reproductions of the splendid portrait and selling them to admirers of President Washington all over the world. He obtained permission from the owner of the portrait —not the artist—to make an engraved likeness of it. Soon after, Mr. Washington died and there could not have been a better time for Heath to launch the sale of his engravings to a grief-stricken public.

The birthplace of the famed artist, so carefully preserved all the years since he lived there and so lovingly restored by neighbors and public-spirited citizens of the community in which it stands, is now open to the public and has recently been designated by the U. S. Department of the Interior as a National Historic Site. The house is a simple gambrel-roofed, low-ceilinged red cottage situated beside a tiny stream near the head of the Pettaquamscott River. The fireplace hearths are wide, the furnishings are simple, and the stairs descending to the cellar are steep and narrow. They lead to the room in which Gilbert Stuart's father first made a living when he came as a young man to this country from Scotland, for he was a snuff miller.

This snuff mill turned out to be an unsuccessful venture and the young Scot moved his wife and three young children across Narragansett Bay to Newport, where he had friends to help him reestablish his trade of grinding and selling snuff in a more prosperous location.

Newport even in the eighteenth century was attractive to people of leisure and wealth, as it was a seaport town and its location was naturally beautiful. Here young Gilbert Stuart for the first time went to public schools, and here, too, for the first time, he was exposed to the thing that interested him most—the art of drawing and painting. He became so skilled that as a youngster he was given his first commission by Dr. William Hunter to paint a picture of two dogs. This picture hangs in the historic Hunter house in Newport today. At the early age of thirteen he was given an order to paint two portraits, from a Mr. and Mrs. John Bannister.

There came to Newport a Scottish artist named Cosmo Alexander, who took an interest in our young painter. The two returned to Scotland together with a plan intended to give Gilbert an opportunity to study painting. Unfortunately Alexander died soon after, leaving the young American alone and destitute. He returned to Newport, working his passage on a collier, which was so dreadful an experience that he could never afterward be induced to speak of it.

At home again, he began to receive commissions for painting portraits, which he particularly loved to do, and was paid liberally enough for them that by 1775 he had saved money for a return to London. Uninterested in the political situation, which was becoming acute in America, his one goal was to find the opportunity to study and paint. He landed in London, where for a time he played the organ in a small church for his livelihood, as he was gifted in music as well as painting. He introduced himself to another American living there, Benjamin West, who was well established as a painter in the best circles of society. West gave him every encouragement by taking him into his home as a helper and student, and soon Gilbert Stuart was attracting attention in portraiture.

One day a Scottish gentleman named William Grant came to Gilbert's studio to sit for a portrait he had commissioned the artist to do. It was a very cold day, and Mr. Grant remarked that the weather was better suited to ice skating than portrait-sitting. Gilbert agreed, and having been a good skater as a boy in Rhode Island, invited his client to join him at a pond nearby where they attracted considerable attention by their skill. When they returned to the studio, Stuart painted Mr. Grant full length as he had seen him skating at the pond. This painting was publicly exhibited at a Royal Academy show and attracted so much attention that when Mr. Grant visited the exhibition he was closely followed by the crowds who easily recognized him, and in embarrassment he left. This portrait of Mr. Grant now hangs in the National Gallery of Art in Washington, D.C.—a splendid full-length painting of a gentleman of such elegance, aplomb, and good-natured snobbishness so obviously enjoying himself that I visit it at every opportunity. The portrait is simply known as "The Skater."

Gilbert Stuart was now well established as a painter of portraits. Hitherto denied the opportunities for good living which he apparently cherished, he began spending his earnings lavishly on good food, fine clothes, and entertaining. He married Miss Charlotte Coates, the daughter of a physician, who shared Gilbert's love for music and gaiety. The marriage was opposed by Miss Coates's family, who were fond of the attractive young painter, but thought him a poor financial risk because of his spendthrift ways. They were right.

In 1787, at the height of his success and popularity in London, and with excellent prospects there for the future, he fled to Ireland to evade his creditors, for by this time he was spending his money much faster than he could make it. Added to his extravagance was his lack of business acumen. He is said to have kept no books, and was always in financial difficulties to the end of his days. In Ireland, he continued to be successful as a painter. He must have painted a good many portraits of fashionable Irishmen, but there is very little record of them. A search for them there might be interesting and fruitful. Stuart continued to entertain lavishly, spending foolishly. Eventually he was forced also to flee Ireland and return to his own country.

He lived in New York, in Philadelphia (then the seat of the Federal government), and in Boston, and in his remaining lifetime was to paint many portraits of the most fashionable Americans.

It had been his hope and wish to establish a substantial living when he returned to his own country by painting portraits of George Washington. He was introduced to the President by John Jay, and in 1795 Washington sat for his first portrait. This painting was copied a number of times by Stuart himself, but he was dissatisfied with the original painting and eventually destroyed it. The picture came to be known as "The Vaughan Portrait" from one of the owners of a Stuart-painted copy, and the view is of the right side of Washington's face.

In 1796 Stuart painted the full-length Lansdowne portrait of Washington, of which I have already told the story. The engravings made by Heath had an unprecedented sale in this country and in London, but at a time when Stuart needed money—as indeed he always did—the artist himself received for this work only the amount originally paid for the portrait, which was six hundred dollars.

A pair of portraits, consisting of a head of Washington and a companion portrait of Martha, were painted in Germantown, near Philadelphia, where Gilbert had moved his family. This portrait shows the left view of Washington's face. Stuart painted and sold many copies of this Washington portrait, one of which now hangs in Mount Vernon, but as long as he lived, he kept the originals of both portraits which he never completely finished. They were virtually his only legacy to his wife and children when he died in Boston some years later. They were finally bought from Mrs. Stuart by the Boston Athenaeum for fifteen hundred dollars and they now hang in the Boston Museum of Fine Arts.

Gilbert Stuart was an artist of great renown even in his own time because of his ability to interpret so accurately the character and facial features of his subjects in a style very much his own. His portraits usually had simple backgrounds, as he only enjoyed painting the heads and faces of his clients. It was thought by his contemporaries that had he not lived such a socially busy and extravagant life, he might have been an even greater artist, for some thought he failed to exert or produce his fullest effort. He was so sure of his own genius that he seldom signed a painting.

He was eccentric, but a gentleman of elegant and proud bearing. He was clever in conversation, a man of sparkling wit and amusing to his friends and his clients. A box of snuff was his constant companion, and he loved wine to excess. He was a spendthrift, careless in personal financial matters, and left his family wholly unprovided for. But Gilbert Stuart's works are the most reproduced paintings the world has ever seen—for every one-dollar bill circulated bears an engraved adaptation of a Washington portrait by Stuart as does the American two-cent stamp. And there are all those paintings that Stuart himself copied from his originals. His own purse was always empty but the world is enriched through his talent.

> For Age and Want save while you may;
> No morning Sun lasts a whole Day.
> —POOR RICHARD

MAY

Birthstone and Birthdays

May's Birthstone is the *Emerald,* for *Happiness.*

1	16
2	17
3	18
4	19
5	20
6	21
7	22
8	23
9	24
10	25
11	26
12	27
13	28
14	29
15	30
	31

Flower

THE BLUE VIOLET
Viola odorata

Violet is for Faithfulness,
Which in me shall abide;
Hoping, likewise, that from your heart
You will not let it slide.

SOME floral interpreters give to the Violet the meaning of Faithfulness, as Sarah Hale's sonnet suggests; and some give to it a meaning of Modesty. Whichever meaning is preferred by you, gentle reader, shall suffice.

Were Violets especially made for picking? The flowers which appear in such abundance in spring must have been created to gather, for it is the later inconspicuous blooms, hidden in shy modesty under the leaves, which produce the seeds for propagation.

If I were to name the one flower of my childhood which has been most endearing in memory, it would be the Violet, which I gathered in great fragrant bouquets along country roads with my playmates Robert and Paul carrying granite-colored buckets of water in which to keep them fresh. Later, during the war, I gathered the largest Blue Violets with the longest stems I have ever seen, along the banks of the Wabash River in Indiana. Seeds and plants of some of these Violets, brought home, have flourished under the stone walls of my New England garden and have been faithful in providing color and sweet fragrance for many years.

Violets are at home in damp woods, meadows, and gardens of New England as in other places across the country. There are many kinds and many colors, and a collection of Violets makes a choice corner in the garden. The crisp heart-shaped leaves provide a green groundcover for shady places under trees and in woodsy corners. And the neat little plants covered with blue flowers in springtime fill the same corners with blossom to enhance flowering bulbs.

> The violet loves a sunny bank,
>   The cowslip loves the lea;
> The scarlet creeper loves the elm,
>   But I love—thee.
>   —BAYARD TAYLOR, "Proposal"

Bird

THE ORIOLE
Icterus galbula

One of the ones that Midas touched
Who failed to touch us all,
Was that confiding prodigal,
The blissful oriole.

—EMILY DICKINSON

HE IS a great showman. He wears a brilliant, flashing coat, is handsome and debonair; and he has a great repertoire of beautiful songs which he shares with us freely in a rich baritone voice. His disposition is good and he is a dedicated family man. His wife is one of the great builders and architects of the world of nature. It follows that with so many gifts and graces, the Orioles are among New England's most welcome summer inhabitants.

The Baltimore Oriole acquired his name, according to legend, when Lord Baltimore, tired and discouraged from unsuccessful attempts to establish a colony in the New World in the early seventeenth century, finally arrived in Virginia and then accepted the responsibility of building the colony of Maryland. He was so cheered and encouraged by the flashing color and the gaiety of song of the Orioles he found in the trees of the new land that he adopted their colors—black and orange—for the Maryland escutcheon, and called the bird by his own title. The Baltimore Oriole is naturally, then, the state bird of Maryland. He spends his summers in the north, coming to

New England about the first of May and raising a family; and he travels to Central and South America for his winter holiday.

In New England, this splendid bird is sometimes called the "golden robin" and sometimes "firebird." Henry David Thoreau thought the Oriole said "Eat it, Potter, eat it," but the extravagant flutelike song actually varies considerably so that it is difficult to accurately translate it.

The male Oriole arrives a week or so ahead of the female, who travels with her female companions at leisure, and by the first week or so of May, he will issue a loud clear note as if to say "Here . . . here . . . I'm here."

The female Oriole is the contractor and builder of the home, which is the best constructed and most ingeniously made nest of the New England bird families. It consists of a basketlike pouch stoutly anchored to a cluster of twigs at the end of a long branch, usually of an elm tree or a tall maple, oak, or hickory. The wind rocks the swaying branch while the parents croon a lullaby to the young in the nest. It is built into so clever a pouch that other birds are unable to reach the eggs or the young birds, and thus it becomes a mighty fortress for the little family.

The nest is intricately woven of old grass, weed stalks, plant fibers, and sometimes pieces of cloth or string. Inside it is made soft and comfortable by additions of plant down and fine grass, truly a piece of exquisite handiwork. Neither rain nor sun nor wind penetrates its fine construction.

In the cherry tree the Orioles that come to our garden always find a generous swatch of light-colored string and yarn available for use in their nest-building. The pieces of string so donated are rather short—six to eight inches long—so that they will be easy to weave and will not become entangled in branches and twigs.

The nest will usually produce one brood of four to six white eggs which are scrawled with black. The mother looks after the young birds, going into the nest headfirst, then righting herself and peering out of the top as if to make sure she has not been spied upon. She is less colorful than the male,

with olive, yellow, brown, and white in her dress. Her alarm note is a loud
rattle, and neither of the parent birds will hesitate to attack with vigor an
approaching enemy.

Orioles love to sing, loud and clear, from the very tip of the tallest tree.
They flash in and out of the garden, feeding copiously on grubs, caterpillars,
wasps, spiders, grasshoppers, and nests of worms, often announcing a juicy
find with a triumphant call. Occasionally they land in the pea patch and
by splitting the pods gorge on the neat rows of fresh green peas within.

These glowing birds especially appreciate our cherry trees, where their
color splashes brilliantly against the white clouds of blossoms in spring. There
is something in the blossoms they enjoy eating, perhaps the honey, perhaps
the bees, perhaps even the petals. When the cherries are ripe, they look over
the abundant supply of fruit, choose carefully, and fly away with the pur-
loined cherries, possibly to feed the young in the nest, but often to lunch
al fresco in the leafy bower of the elm tree.

There have been years when the Orioles have sung so persistently from
the elm tree that we were sure their nest was hidden among the branches,
yet we were unable to see it, so well was its location concealed, until the
leaves of the tree had withered and blown away in autumn. Even through
autumn storm and winter snow and wind, an Oriole's nest will often resist
the weather's attempts to dislodge it, and it may occasionally be found,
battered and torn, still partly clinging to its branch when spring arrives.

> Hush, 'tis he!
> My Oriole, my glance of summer fire,
> Is come at last; and ever on the watch,
> Twitches the pack-thread I had lightly wound
> About the bough to help his housekeeping.
>
> —JAMES RUSSELL LOWELL

Every Leaf a Miracle

"Sing a song of Spring," cried the sunshine of May,
And the whole world into blossom burst in one delightful day,
The patient apple trees blushed bright in clouds of rosy red,
And the dear birds sang with rapture in the blue sky overhead.

—CELIA THAXTER

MAY DAY has been celebrated merrily for many ages, from fertility festivals of the ancient Egyptians, and feasts of the Romans in honor of their goddess Flora, to the Middle Ages when the people of the British Isles danced about Maypoles. The English decked their villages with flowers and danced in the streets with gay abandon, greatly encouraged by enthusiastic drinking and feasting. In New England the first settlers, the Pilgrims, did not believe in such pagan festivities, and there was no thought of celebrating May Day until one boisterous Thomas Morton set foot on the shores of Boston Bay. He and his crew set up a Maypole on May Day 1627, celebrating their arrival with dancing and other raucous revelry. The Maypole is said to have been a pine tree eighty feet tall wreathed with wild flowers, vines, and ribbons, and adorned with poems especially composed for the occasion. The merriment shocked Governor Bradford and his Puritan followers. Further celebrations of May Day in New England were abandoned until the nineteenth century when children played at dancing around the Maypole and renewed the old, old custom of filling May Baskets with flowers and candies for their friends.

Within the last century or so, New Englanders discovered the delightful practice of serving May Breakfasts, which custom persists to this day. Church guilds, volunteer fire departments, and other groups seeking ways to raise funds for their organizations rise long before dawn to prepare the hearty and now traditional breakfasts which they serve to those who arrive before the workday begins, usually from six to nine o'clock. Fishermen's breakfasts are also served at even earlier, predawn hours on the opening day of the fishing season. And there are many gracious New England hostesses who invite friends for a sociable May Breakfast in their homes to celebrate the spirit of the Merry Month of May at a more leisurely hour. Food for all these breakfast feasts varies considerably, in some cases including an ample slice of homemade pie, that good New England breakfast staple.

In Hanover, New Hampshire, high on the banks of the Connecticut River which forms the boundary between Vermont and New Hampshire (this length of the river legally belongs to New Hampshire) the area alumnae of Mount Holyoke, Simmons, Smith, Vassar, and Wellesley colleges will have spent the whole year gathering secondhand books from their friends, neighbors, well-wishers, and families. They classify the books, price each one, and the first week in May hold a three-day sale to increase scholarship funds for girls going to these colleges, sharing the proceeds equally among their five alumnae clubs in the Hanover area. They take over an auditorium on the Dartmouth College campus and spread out the books according to content: history, poetry, art, cookery, travel, drama, biography, novels, whodunits. There are sets of encyclopedias, Harvard Classics, and Stoddard's lectures. In the gallery is the "all you can carry for fifty cents" department. On the first day of the sale, children are admitted for two hours. On the second day in the morning, book dealers sweep away many of the valuables. Then the public is admitted; and on the last day of the sale everything left is half-price. An annual May event, the sale gets donations from all over New England and eager customers from as far away as can conveniently drive to Hanover.

At Jamaica Plain in Boston, the Arnold Arboretum plays host in mid-May to many thousands who come to see the incomparable Arboretum display of over five hundred varieties of lilacs in full bloom. It is one of the best flower shows in the country, in a setting planned for superb effects of color and texture.

If there is told somewhere the story of how the first lilac came to this country, I have not found it, but the shrub was undoubtedly brought by one whose European garden had been enhanced by lilacs. Now, not only in the arboretums, parks, and formal gardens of New England, but in dooryards over its length and breadth, the lilac blooms in its beauty. It is the state flower of New Hampshire. One who takes a drive on almost any back road will find great thickets of old lilacs growing beside the cellar holes or old barn foundations of long-gone farms. Driving on a sunny spring day when lilacs are in bloom one sees them growing beside kitchen doors, shading garden walks, sheltering the weathered clapboards of ancient buildings, crowding stone walls and fences and country roadsides with color and fragrance. In many colonial dooryards, the lilac was often the only shrub, planted there by flower-hungry farm or village wives who were well rewarded by the grateful hum of bees, by the birds who nestled in the shelter of the branches, by the armloads of fragrant flowers which they could put into a pitcherful of water on their kitchen tables.

Do you know Walt Whitman's poem "When Lilacs Last in the Dooryard Bloom'd"? It was written after the death of President Lincoln, and these lines from it picture perfectly the old familiar shrub:

> In the door-yard, fronting an old farm-house, near the
>   whitewash'd palings,
> Stands the lilac bush, tall-growing, with heart-shaped
>   leaves of rich green,

With many a pointed blossom, rising, delicate, with the
    perfume strong I love,
With every leaf a miracle . . . and from this bush in the
    door-yard,
With delicate-color'd blossoms, and heart-shaped leaves
    of rich green,
A sprig, with its flower, I break.

In some parts of the world, May Day has taken on political overtones. But in the New England countryside it is a day of observance of the arrival of real spring. Here it is still the time when we realize that suddenly the days are longer and brighter and warmer; the trees and lawns are greener, and the smell of the dew-laden spring flowers is sweet. The early morning mist rises with the sun over the east field, curling like smoke to disappear into the trees and the warming blue sky. The early birds in all their glorious caroling sing from almost every treetop. Bees buzz in full-blown orchards. Listen a moment to the sound of insects, humming, buzzing, singing. There is a spreading of gay color across valleys and hills—blends of green, red buds of maple, dripping golden tassels of willow branches. The deep blue of spring skies is puffed with featherbed clouds. Every path we take is embroidered in flowers: violets and wild ginger and bloodroot and spring beauty and trillium and jack-in-the-pulpit and ladies' slipper and the sweet Mayflower, the trailing arbutus.

Birds looking for nesting materials are pulling frantically at weed stems and other stringy things. In a small net bag, such as onions or grapefruit come in, we put feathers, clean combings from the dog's daily brushing (soft and light, they make lovely nest linings), any bunches of tiny dried rootlets that we may have unearthed in the garden. We stack small twigs for the wrens to find. By the end of the season most of the material will have disappeared. We like to think it makes contented tenants of our bird-houses to have given this help and attention to their building problems.

The compost pile is now rich in humus ready for potting, for digging into flower beds, for enriching the kitchen garden. Even the snake which lives in the warmth of the bottom of the pile is a harbinger of spring, lively and wriggling as we disturb his morning nap. One year we uncovered a clutch of snake eggs, white rubbery eggs which stuck together. Experimentally we squeezed one to see what would happen. Out popped a snake about four inches long and as big around as the stem of a dandelion flower, and it scuttled into the shelter of the stone wall as if it had always lived there.

With spade and fork and rake we go over the rich soil in the old barn foundation where annuals and salad vegetables are planted. In spite of the many times the ground has been turned over in spring, we still uncover relics of the kitchen midden of days gone by—pieces of broken bottles, bits of old crockery and dishes, part of a lady's brooch, rusted ancient hand tools and handmade nails, once a whole milk-glass egg and a brown whiskey bottle with the sheaf-of-wheat design.

Garden peas and sweet peas are the first to go into the mellow soil, then lettuce and radish seed. Late in the month other seeds are planted, tomato plants set in place, gladioli and dahlias planted deep. Some country folk still do their planting by the phases of the moon, but we had a neighbor who followed this caprice and the fickleness of New England weather sometimes found him waiting until late June for a good dry day at the proper moon phase. In such years, he would be privileged to share his neighbor's corn in the late summer and fall when his own failed to mature before early frosts. So a better motto might be to plant when you and the weather and the ground are ready, never mind the moon. However, no New Englander who lives inland or northerly will plant tomatoes and tender seedlings until Decoration Day if he can help it, the usual late-frost deadline.

The herb garden is ready for seed-planting of its annuals; on Decoration

Day we set in the perennial plants we have bought or raised from seed. The little wheel garden looks charming and we are eager for the first harvest of leaf or sprig or branch or seed for the kitchen and for potpourri.

After a vigorous morning of work in the garden, there is time after lunch for exploring in the spring sunshine among the blossoming apple trees, down the lane, into the woods, through the old graveyard at the bottom of the Bog Road. Armed with a basket, a trowel, a sharp knife, and a pair of clippers, we find great treasures on such a stroll—an unusual stone glittering with mica or lumpy with garnets to tuck into the rock garden, some acorns, perhaps a little handful of Mayflower blossoms which we carefully clip from the trailing stems. In each different kind of woods environment there is a suitable flower. Under the hemlocks thrive the Mayflower and ladies' slipper; at the edge of the bog is the pinxter flower or wild azalea; different kinds of violets grow in many different localities. Some of these lovelies we dig carefully from our own woods if the supply is ample and if we can get a good trowelful of the deep woodsy soil surrounding each plant. We take them back to our own "Fern Valley," a little shady piece of rich earth near the barn where we once found a dump of old tin cans and discarded miscellany from the barn workshop.

This wild garden is not as ambitious or as complete or as beautiful as the lovely Fern Valley located on the grounds of our National Arboretum in Washington, D.C., but in a much smaller way has a somewhat comparable history. In that Fern Valley, which belongs to all of us in America who love wild natural plants, a tiny winding brook and its surroundings were reclaimed by a group of devoted garden club members. They donned blue jeans and sneakers, and provided themselves with shovels and spades and trowels. They begged help from the Arboretum to clear the debris of many years which had been dumped along the woodland stream gulley by the farmers who had once owned the land. They begged the gift of plants from many sources, including wild-flower nurseries and preserves of New

England. In Fern Valley are now found wildlings indigenous to the East Coast, all inconspicuously identified. There are delightful paths to follow, benches for an occasional quiet rest, picnic tables in a suitable place for those who wish to spend plenty of time in this lovely retreat, and even guides on certain occasions, these same devoted garden club members. Here has been created by hard-working ladies in a miniature woodland, a nature sanctuary of incredible beauty and interest where once existed an unsightly farm dump full of rusted machinery, tools, and old cars.

No, our own wild-flower garden is not so grand, but it provides moments of real delight. We can take a moment each day to enjoy its magic as each flower opens its rare blossom and each fern unfolds.

As we turn homeward from a springtime walk, we watch the paths and the ditches and the fields for spring greens for supper. At the edge of the trees near Stirrup Iron Brook are the watercress, and the fiddlehead ferns. With sharp knife we cut a dozen tightly curled fern fronds, fresh as the rushing cold waters of the brook, to clean, cook, and serve as a vegetable. As we cross the North Field, there are bushels of dandelions for the taking, dandelions in plenty, rich in vitamins and iron. Many people can them, but we are content to dig a "mess" now and then of full tender plants with buds just appearing in the center of the leaf cluster. They will make a delicious salad, or may be cooked as greens with a touch of salt pork to add flavor.

Stalks of pieplant, or rhubarb, growing richly behind the barn, are pulled and will make the first fresh pie or sauce of the season. Rhubarb is treated as a fruit, since it really acts and tastes like it when cooked; but in reality it is a vegetable. Our grandmothers considered it a good spring tonic and it does have certain laxative qualities. It is so delicious that it should not suffer the indignity of being treated as a medicine. The first tender stems pulled in May are the best. The season never seems long enough, for by the Fourth of July stalks get tougher. In order to give the roots time and strength for next year's crop, the Fourth is a good date to give up pulling rhubarb stalks for the summer.

One of the pleasures of May is fishing from the covered bridge, the hidden covered bridge which knows but little traffic these days. It crosses a rushing mountain river, but the road it accommodates no longer goes any-where. Armed with our fishing licenses, worms ("night crawlers") dug out of the depths of the compost pile, a hook, a line, and a sinker, we take off as early as possible (not very early at that), and in no time we are leaning over the side of the bridge through a convenient gap in the weathered boards.

There is the pungent sweet fragrance of spring in the soft air, the fra-grance of damp deep natural humus, of blossoming native trees and shrubs in the cool shade on the banks of the river, the musky smell of a nearby skunk cabbage patch. There is music in the soft air, too, the music of ruffled waters eddying over rocks, of birds singing in the treetops, of the menacing hum of blackflies around our eyes and ears.

Waiting is rewarded by a fast tug that means a trout on the hook, there is a whisk of shining silver in the water, the taut line, the bent pole. The first trout we land each year is a special triumph and a special treat for supper when sautéed in butter with a half-teaspoon of finely chopped fennel sprin-kled over. To go with it, a good country cook will have dandelion greens; or a fresh salad of any crisp greens from the field or stream such as sorrel, watercress, chicory, mustard, cowslips (marsh marigold), or plantain.

DANDELION GREENS

Dig a large basketful of greens before the blossoms open, when young and tender. Cut out any buds, cut off roots and damaged leaves. Wash thoroughly in cold water and shake off excess water.

Put 2 cups of water in a large kettle and bring to a brisk boil. Put the greens into a steamer basket and then into the boiling water. Boil 10 minutes; drain the leaves and change the water in the kettle. When the second water is boiling, again put in the greens and add 2 or 3 inch-cubed pieces of salt pork. Cook until greens are tender (about 12 to 15 minutes). Drain well. Can be chopped or left whole. Butter, salt, and pepper may be added when fully cooked, instead of the salt pork. A garnish of chopped crisp bacon and sliced hard-cooked eggs is very good.

DANDELION WINE

Instead of worrying about the dandelions which bloom in our lawns, we might consider them a special bounty. Most flower wines are delicious; dandelion wine is no exception.

Pick 8 quarts of dandelion flowers fully open, without any part of the stem. Wash thoroughly in cold water. Put them into a large clean crock and pour over them 2 gallons of fresh water which has been brought to a boil in an enamel kettle (never use metalware in making wine). Cover the crock and let it stand at "room temperature" (around 65–70°) for three or four days. Stir several times a day with a long wooden paddle or spoon.

Strain the liquid back into the enamel kettle, squeezing the flowers to extract all the juice. Wash and cut thin peel from 4 oranges and 4 lemons and put the peel into the kettle. Add 5 pounds of sugar and stir to dissolve. Bring this to a boil and simmer for 30 minutes. Add a cup of water to replace the liquid which will have evaporated. Pour back into the clean crock. Add 4 cups of chopped white raisins and the juice from the lemons and oranges.

In ½ cup of warm water, dissolve 2 yeast cakes and add this to the liquid in the crock. Cover crock and return to its room-temperature storage place (we keep ours in the Butt'ry, of course) and let the brew ferment for up to three weeks, or until the bubbling of fermentation ceases.

Strain carefully through folded cheesecloth into clean glass gallon jars and set aside for two weeks to clear. At this point, there will be sediment in the bottom of the jars, so the clear liquid should be carefully siphoned off (or removed with a ladle) and bottled. The rest may be strained again once or twice until quite clear and then bottled. Cork when bottled.

Dandelion wine is best kept for at least a year before drinking. It is delicious served quite cold at tea time or with dessert, or as refreshment for special company.

SPRING GREENS SALAD

Dig very young dandelions when buds are still tiny. Cut mustard greens at ground level before growth begins to lengthen. Cut marsh marigolds at ground level when flower buds are just opening. Cut watercress close to roots. Remove all roots, damaged leaves, and tough stems. Wash greens well in cold water, dry, and chill in plastic bags.

In the bottom of a wooden salad bowl, rub cut halves of a garlic bud. To serve 4 people, tear about half a small head of fresh lettuce into the bowl. Add native greens of your choice. Using a wooden salad serving spoon, pour olive oil over the greens, using about two spoonfuls. Toss carefully so that all leaves are coated with oil. Into the same spoon, pour a little salt (about a teaspoonful) and grind pepper to your taste over it, then fill the spoon with tarragon vinegar or good cider vinegar. With the serving fork, mix the vinegar, salt, and pepper in the spoon, then pour over the lettuce and toss again to mix well. Add more vinegar if you like a tart salad. Or make Greene Herb Gardens special dressing, perfect for spring greens. Enjoy, identify, and compare the flavor of each green, remembering how filled with iron and valuable vitamins are these fresh greens of field and stream.

GREENE HERB GARDENS DRESSING FOR FRESH SPRING GREENS

8 Tbs. salad oil	2½ drops Tabasco sauce
2 Tbs. vinegar (tarragon if possible)	½ tsp. mixture of dried or fresh herbs, chopped fine
2 Tbs. water	¼ tsp. salt
1 clove diced garlic	Dash of fresh-ground pepper
½ tsp. brown sugar	

Combine all ingredients and shake well before using.

FIDDLEHEAD FERNS

The ferns which are most commonly used for Fiddlehead Greens are those of the *Osmunda* classification: the Interrupted, the Royal, and the Cinnamon ferns, all of which bear quite thick growths of protective hair on the fiddleheads and must be scraped. Also used are the heads of the graceful and tall Ostrich Fern. A gentleman we know who is versed in country things says that the common Bracken is the best one to use for greens, as there is no thick hair to be cleaned. The Bracken heads, however, are small and delicate and it takes a great many to make a serving.

Our favorite Fiddleheads are made from the shoots of the Ostrich Fern. They should be gathered when they are 3 or 4 inches tall and still tightly curled. The name Fiddleheads, of course, comes from this early stage of their development when the curled fronds do indeed look like the curled head of a fiddle.

They should be cut, like asparagus, just before preparing them for cooking so as to be absolutely fresh in flavor. Wash the heads, carefully unrolling them (being watchful not to break them off in this process) just enough to remove sand, scales, and hair with the fingers or a small paring knife. Put the cleaned heads in a steamer basket and lower into kettle with

1 cup rapidly boiling water. Cover the kettle and steam for 20 to 30 minutes or until tender (it takes less time when they are fresh-picked). Drain, salt and pepper lightly, and put into a serving dish. May be served as a vegetable with a simple lemon butter sauce and garnished with sliced hard-cooked eggs; or serve on buttered toast with a little melted butter poured over.

The Dandelion
With locks of gold to-day;
Tomorrow, silver gray;
Then blossom-bald. Behold,
Oh man, thy fortune told!
—JOHN B. TABB

Portrait—Ernest Henry Wilson

ARISTOCRAT OF THE GARDENS

"A BIT of beautiful New England forever preserved as a garden in which is planted all that is hardy among woody plants. A garden of trees and shrubs assembled together from the uttermost parts of the northern hemisphere and open free to all every day in the year. A garden where bosky hills, wooded knolls, steep cliffs, open meadows and valleys are fragrant with the odors of foliage, flower and fruit. A garden where the birds may breed unmolested and where they can find food in abundance at all seasons of the year."

Everyone who lives in New England has such a garden; it is indeed ours to enjoy at every season of the year. At lilac time it would seem that we are all in the garden at once to wander along the grassy paths absorbing the sweet fragrance of the lilacs and the fullness of spring, but there are many who enjoy the beauties of the garden just as much at any other time of year.

"The garden," of course, is the Arnold Arboretum in Boston. The description above was written about the Arboretum by Dr. Ernest Henry Wilson in his book *America's Greatest Garden.* Hundreds of acres of rich grass, trees, and shrubs grow luxuriantly in a natural setting of incomparable beauty. And it will be so for a thousand years, then another thousand years, and so on forever, according to the terms under which the Arboretum was created.

Originally a plot of but one hundred twenty-five acres known as the Bussey Farm, the Arboretum was created in 1872 through the generosity of

Mr. James Arnold, a merchant of New Bedford, Massachusetts. The trust which was set up to provide for the Arboretum was turned over to Harvard College, Dr. Charles Sprague Sargent was appointed director, the city of Boston was persuaded to add land and maintenance, and the Arboretum was on its way to becoming one of the finest public gardens in the world.

At first, only plants from North America suitable to the Boston climate were considered as subjects for Arboretum culture. Gradually, seeds and plants from other areas were included. But it was not until 1906 that the Arboretum ventured into worldwide plant-hunting, when Dr. Sargent persuaded Mr. Ernest Henry Wilson of Kew Gardens in England to join his staff for the purpose of gathering plants and seeds from far corners of the earth.

Ernest Henry Wilson was chosen for this venturesome activity because, although a young man, he had already proved himself in the field of botany and horticulture as a lecturer, teacher, and plant-hunter. It was a field that was completely natural and fitting for him. He was to make such valuable contributions to the collections of the Arnold Arboretum and the gardens of America that their value can hardly be estimated.

Although he was born in England, at Chipping Camden in Gloucestershire, on February 15, 1876, Ernest Henry Wilson was adopted by New England, and he in turn adopted New England so thoroughly that his name will forever be linked with many of our favorite garden plants. On a leisurely walk through the Arboretum, or one's own garden, we can easily find many plants which he brought to us from the wilds of Asia—the Regal Lily, the Tea Crabapple, the *Cotoneaster apiculata* ("Rock spray" cotoneaster), the Korean Box, the Beauty Bush, and many others.

The story is told of his first journey to China, where he was sent by an English nursery to hunt for the *Davidia involucrata*, or Dove Tree, which had been seen there by another plant-hunter. Wilson made the complicated arrangements for this, his first, perilous trip into the wilds, having learned the approximate location of the object of his search. He spent months of hardship traveling the dangerous course of the Yangtze River into the mountainous reaches of China. At one point, his boat overturned and he lost much of his photographic equipment, including negatives which he had obtained with difficulty. At last he reached the spot where the Dove Tree was reported to grow. Imagine his disappointment to find that the tree had been cut down; only a stump remained. The journey did have a happy ending, however, for in another location he came upon several trees from which he could obtain seed. These seeds were germinated successfully and the Dove Tree is now rather widely distributed in gardens of the Northern Hemisphere.

When Wilson returned to England from this trip he was married to Miss Ellen Ganderton. To them was born a daughter, Muriel Primrose, named for her father's favorite flower. Wilson made another trip into the Szechwan Province of China, then in 1906, Dr. Sargent of the Arnold Arboretum persuaded him to come to Boston.

In January 1907, Wilson set out again for China, this time for the Arboretum, to locate trees and shrubs which might be particularly suited to growing in the gardens of America. He located a number of interesting conifers, but happened upon them during a year when they did not bear seed. He also saw glorious fields of the Regal Lily, although he did not this time collect a bulb of it to bring back. In 1910 another journey was arranged, and once again he ventured into the high mountains of western China. This time he collected many bulbs of the now-famous Regal Lily, Sargent's Lily, the Wilmott Lily, and many other plants of importance in our gardens, as well as seeds of the conifers he had previously sought.

On this trip, an accident occurred which was nearly disastrous. A planthunting expedition was dangerous at best, and Wilson had ventured into some of the most inaccessible places in the world. He had every confidence in his guides and bearers and they in him. But as he was beginning his homeward journey, he was caught by a landslide, which resulted in his leg being broken by a falling rock. As he lay pinned to the ground, a team of forty mules came rushing down the mountain path. But each one stepped over him completely, so that not one hoof touched him. He was carried by his bearers on a stretcher for many days over the mountain trails to a medical missionary's camp, where he was treated. The leg did not heal well, and it was many months after he reached Boston before he recovered the use of it. He was left with one leg shorter than the other, and was required to wear a special shoe to compensate for it. He always seemed unsure of the strength of the crushed leg. This may have contributed, many years later, to an even more disastrous accident.

Wilson was a fearless explorer, and an able administrator. In all his foreign travels, he had no difficulties with his native guides, who respected and revered him. He was proud of his nickname, "Chinese" Wilson, for he admired the Chinese people and made friends with them easily. He was a shy and modest man and seldom talked of his many adventures, accomplishments, and travels.

Upon returning to the Arboretum with his new plant discoveries, he was always meticulous in cataloging, naming, and describing them for the records. As a lecturer, Wilson was especially popular, for he had a way of explaining difficult horticultural terms in an easy manner which his audience enjoyed. Scheduled to speak one evening to people with gardening and horticultural interests, he saw before him a great bouquet of mixed garden flowers. When it came his turn to speak, he cast aside his prepared talk, and choosing the flowers one by one from the arrangement on the table, he told the story of their discovery and development in such a way that he held his audience spellbound and enchanted with his reminiscences.

In addition to his China trips, Wilson went to Japan, from where he brought back to us the lovely Kurume azaleas, as well as cherries, and other plants; to Korea; and to Formosa, where he searched for plants under difficulties among the headhunting tribes of the island. By 1919, upon his return to Boston, he was made assistant director of the Arnold Arboretum. The following year he embarked on yet another journey, this time to visit many other countries of the world on a good-will mission, to encourage a free exchange of horticultural information and plant materials among the countries he visited. This journey was to be of great value to botanists in all the countries involved.

In 1927, Ernest Henry Wilson was made "Keeper" of the Arboretum, a title he chose himself, after the death of Director Sargent. At last he could devote the time necessary to writing about the many plants he had discovered. His constant aim was to stimulate a greater interest among Americans in gardening; to encourage nurserymen to grow more and better plants; and to improve garden planning generally. As an advisory editor of *Horticulture Magazine,* he was able to develop many of his ideas for its readers.

In all, Ernest Henry Wilson had collected about sixteen thousand herbarium specimens and over five thousand photographs of plants and their natural environment; had introduced here more than a thousand botanical species which had never before been cultivated outside their native location; had written twelve books and hundreds of magazine articles; and was a popular lecturer. He had many plans for a long, full life of devotion to horticulture and gardening.

Harvard and Trinity colleges bestowed honorary degrees on him, so that he now became Dr. Ernest Henry Wilson, and he was known and warmly regarded everywhere in the plant world, with many other awards to his credit.

On a rainy afternoon in October 1930, Dr. Wilson and his wife Ellen were returning to Boston from a visit with their daughter when their car skidded on wet leaves and plunged forty feet over a steep embankment. They were both killed. No one knows just what happened, but perhaps the leg which had been injured so many years before in the mountains of China could not function with sufficient strength to avert the disastrous skid. The accident brought to an untimely end Ernest Wilson's career of devoted learning and experience in the world of gardens. But the Arnold Arboretum —and in fact, our own private gardens all over America—have been so enriched by his efforts that they will never be lost.

Among his books were several editions of *Aristocrats of the Garden,* and one called *Aristocrats of the Trees.* He was a great lover of trees and believed that "A garden without trees scarcely deserves its name." My own favorite book is *If I Were to Make a Garden,* in which he discussed garden planning, many plants, their history and characteristics, and best of all, the enjoyment of a garden. "There is no royal road or cleancut path to the making of a garden," he directed us, and he avowed that his dream garden would be a natural, not an exotic, garden, where "sweet odors should live beneath my windows. . . . May we foster the love and appreciation of flowers and from them reap the delight that characterized our forefathers." To borrow a term from Dr. Wilson, he himself might be thought of as "The Aristocrat of Gardens."

Apple blossoms, budding, blowing,
    In the soft May air:
Cups with sunshine overflowing—
Flakes of fragrance, drifting, snowing,
Showering everywhere!
                    —LUCY LARCOM

Charles Dudley Warner said: "What a man needs in gardening is a cast-iron back with a hinge in it." He also said: "Lettuce is like conversation: it must be fresh and crisp, so sparkling that you scarcely notice the bitter in it."

CARRY A SUNDAY POSY

JUNE

Birthstone and Birthdays

June's Birthstone is the *Agate,* representing *Purity, Health,* or *Long Life.*

1	16
2	17
3	18
4	19
5	20
6	21
7	22
8	23
9	24
10	25
11	26
12	27
13	28
14	29
15	30

Flower

THE ROSE
Rosa

ONE can express almost any sentiment through a gift of roses, depending on the color or kind, but roses generally have a connotation of love. *The Coloured Language of Flowers*, compiled by a Mrs. Burke in a much earlier era, listed thirty-three kinds of old-fashioned roses, each with a different sentiment, from the Austrian Rose meaning "Thou art all that is lovely," to a White Rose and a Red Rose together, which signified "Unity." One could give a word of warning to a flirt by the gift of a Carolina Rose, which meant "Love is dangerous." Or one could certainly squelch a romance by sending a Japanese Rose, which meant "Beauty is your only attraction." In those romantic, sentimental days, a crown of roses was a "Reward of Virtue." If one just couldn't manage to utter the proper endearing words, a single Moss Rosebud would say it, for this was a simple "Confession of Love." White roses which were included in bridal bouquets, of course meant "Happy Love." Since the gift of a Damask Rose meant "Brilliant Complexion," one can only think it was a delicate suggestion that the lady-love was wearing too much rouge. If she had been unfaithful, one could send her a Yellow Rose which meant "Jealousy," or a Champion Rose to say "Only deserve my love," or as a last resort a York and Lancaster Rose to declare "War."

The name for this flower is basically the same in nearly all languages: Rose, or Rosa, or some kindred word. But to everyone the world over the flower means something beautiful and precious.

A rose is sweet
   No matter where it grows;
But our wild roses, flavored by the sea,
And colored by the salt winds and much sun
To healthiest intensity of bloom—
We think the world has none more beautiful.
                                    —LUCY LARCOM

Bird

I meant to do my work today—
  But a brown bird sang in the appletree,
And a butterfly flitted across the field,
  And all the leaves were calling me.
                    —RICHARD LE GALLIENNE

ON A warm day in June when the breeze is quiet in the garden and the sun is hot on my back, I am easily diverted from chores of planting and weeding to sit on a weathered bench and listen to the gay song of a little brown bird in the apple tree.

For many years, we tried in vain to attract Wrens to the garden, with all manner of neat houses built especially to their size and liking, we thought. Suddenly a pair of Wrens arrived one spring, looked the situation over thoroughly—and built in the open mailbox! Nowadays, we keep the mailbox closed, but the Wrens have returned to us, nesting in the neat little wren-houses scattered about, one of which hangs in an apple tree.

Wrens like to build in anything handy—gourds, flowerpots, even a tin can nailed to a well-shaded post will attract them if the size of the hole is not too great—the size of a quarter is the rule. We even read of a pair of Wrens which built their nest in the sleeve of a ragged jacket worn by a scarecrow in a kitchen garden. This inclination to build in unusual places is well known, as shown in the old limerick:

There was an Old Man with a beard,
Who said: "It is just as I feared!
   Two Owls and a Hen,
    Four Larks and a Wren
Have all built their nests in my beard."

Wrens work with tremendous energy to build their nests of many small twigs. They round the nest out neatly and line it with soft grass or feathers. The male busies himself first, perhaps as a part of the mating ritual, to prepare a suitable dwelling, stuffing in twigs and singing vigorously. Sometimes when a twig is too long to go into the door of his house, he will spend a few seconds maneuvering it, and his antics are comical as he scolds and twists until in triumph he finds a way to get the twig into the opening.

I have watched with wonder as Wrens cleaned out a birdhouse filled with sticks from an old nest, in order to have a place to build their own. They apparently love to build nests, and sometimes, too late in the season for nesting, they seem to enjoy filling a wrenhouse with twigs just for the fun of it. "Busy work," it could be called.

When the female is ready to help with the nest, father gives up his construction work and lets her complete the building. Once the nest is finished and the six to eight tiny speckled eggs are laid, the pair exhibit excellent housekeeping instincts and keep the nest scrupulously clean until the young have flown away.

Jenny Wren, as the bird is affectionately called, is a tiny bird with pert ways and an inquisitive nature. Her back is a warm brown color, the wings are faintly barred with black, and the breast is grayish-white. The bill is rather long and slightly curved; the tail is also quite long and it points saucily upward except when the bird is singing or flying. Wrens are common summer residents of New England, but they can be quite absent from some areas. They migrate south in winter since their food is entirely made up of insects impossible to find here in that season.

Wrens prefer living in dooryards of suburban or country houses. They dart in and out of piles of old leaves, stone walls, and flower beds looking for bugs, slugs, cutworms, and small beetles, and no one could estimate the quantity of insects they consume and feed to their two or three yearly families.

Any threat of danger to their households is met with a harsh chatter of some intensity, and they have been known to plunder the nests of other birds who build too close to their established territory. Except for this protective fighting instinct, they are cheerful, vivacious, friendly little birds of inexhaustible energy.

The Wren's song bubbles with remarkable volume from the tiny throat, like a fountain of melody tumbling in joyful cascades. The song seldom fails to give us pause in the day's work, or to give us a gay lift of spirit.

> Then sing, ye birds,
> Sing, sing a joyous song!
> —WILLIAM WORDSWORTH

Carry a Sunday Posy

My beloved is gone down into his garden, to the beds of spices, to feed in the gardens, and to gather lilies.

—SONG OF SOLOMON

AS I DRIVE along one of New England's highways on a warm day in June, the soft air is often permeated by the lovely woodsy fragrance of sweet fern, which grows abundantly on the gravelly banks at the edge of woods. I like to remember that when the Puritans who founded the colonies at Salem and at Massachusetts Bay first arrived, in each case on a day in June, the fragrance which greeted them was that of sweet fern, and it reminded them of the gardens they had left behind them. "We had now fair Sunshine Weather and so pleasant a Sweet Aire as did much refresh us, and there came a smell off the Shore like the Smell of a Garden," wrote John Winthrop. When they disembarked on the shores of their new land, they breathed deep of this perfume; they gathered the wild strawberries which carpeted the fields and the sweet roses which lined the shore.

Encouraged by these reminders of the homes they had forsaken in a search for freedom, these colonists had soon delegated pastures, laid out their commons (Boston Common is still open for cows to graze one day a year), built their rude cabins, and planted their garden plots. In the land around them, they found herbs for medicine and for cooking, which they gathered in plenty. Seeds and roots brought from their homeland grew and blossomed and were harvested. They gave rightful thanks for their bounty.

At first, in the hearts of the Puritans and in the gardens of New England, there was little room for anything so gay and impractical as flowers. But roses have a way of entrenching themselves in the most surprising places, and soon there were roses growing in the dooryards. And then there came hollyhocks—perhaps a gift of seeds from someone who knew the longing of Puritan wives for something from "home." White daisies growing among the fields of grain, stowaway seeds among the wheat or barley, were gathered eagerly. In the woods were found wild columbine and violets and ferns which could be transplanted into crannies of the vegetable and herb gardens. Every ship dispatched from the old country to these shores was laden with exciting goods, including more seeds and plants from the gardens of Europe. Soon the gardens of the new world offered "fragrant savours and delectable sights" which became more fragrant and delectable as the years went on.

By the middle of the eighteenth century, New England gardens had become increasingly elaborate; some were even being laid out by architects. The first greenhouse in America was built in Boston for Andrew Faneuil. Fruit trees were planted in orchard rows; bee skeps made of ropes of twisted straw housed swarms of useful bees to make honey tasting of lavender, thyme, sweet marjoram, larkspur, lupine, sweet peas, and apple and quince blossoms. In the flower gardens decorative touches appeared with the addition of sundials, garden seats, sometimes fountains, trellises, arbors, and elaborate well- or tool-houses. Many of these gardens were quite formal in design, bordered by walls, fences, hedges, or trees.

Men of New England gathered on their estates all the plants which were of practical use or extraordinary beauty to them, vying with each other or exchanging such plants with each other and with botanists of Europe. Along the seacoast, the gardens of prosperous shipowners and merchants were expanded to hold not only flower beds and orchards of fruit trees, but places to grow melons and cucumbers; small-fruit areas for gooseberries and currants; aviaries for pheasants and peacocks. The first American cookbook, published in Hartford, Connecticut, in 1796, contains directions on "How To Choose a Peacock for Roasting." Dovecotes were often located in the garden near the kitchen door, the better to catch tender squabs.

Colonial men enjoyed walking in and talking about their gardens; their women, even the most genteel and prosperous of them, did their own sowing and planting. It was the thing to do. A fine garden was considered to be a matter of position as well as of practicality in mid-eighteenth-century America. A farmer's garden might have a few things the more formal estates did not have—a haystack, some geese, a few lambs to crop the lawns and to enrich the store of wool and meat. But these gardens, too, were often rather elaborate. A garden became a happy place to be, cheerful and abundantly productive of all that was good in the new land.

The selling of flower seeds was now a business, sometimes indulged in by the lady owners of sundry shops, the seeds being dispensed along with needles, pins, laces, ribbons, and bonnets. Marigold, lobelia, morning glory, larkspur, snapdragon, poppy, amaranth, mignonette, sweet rocket (sometimes called gillyflower), sweet William, baby's breath, Canterbury bell, stock, and many others were now being planted.

In the villages and towns, flowers were planted in the front dooryard to be enjoyed by a neighbor from his window, or by the passersby, little fenced-in enclosures housing the rarest and most treasured of flowers: tulips, narcissi, phlox, and columbine, the London pride, and daylilies, peonies ("pinies"), and flowering almond. The front yard became as much a part of one's housekeeping as the front parlor, and was neat and well kept. There are remnants of these old-fashioned dooryard gardens still to be seen in the villages of New England. Many old lilac and rose and honeysuckle plantings have gained in beauty over the centuries.

The flower gardens of city houses were not in the front dooryards; they were hidden behind the row houses, enclosed with hedges or high vine-covered fences or walls to insure seclusion and privacy from one's neighbors.

On Beacon Hill in Boston, in Newport, or Salem or Portsmouth or many
other cities, such little jewels of gardens may still be seen during spring
house-and-garden tours. I know of one such garden which is still shaded by
a wisteria vine planted two hundred years ago.

All of these old-fashioned gardens had at least two things in common.
They all had roses; they all had herbs. To this day, only the old-fashioned
roses are really at home in most of New England, hardy and reliable. Even
to the Puritans, the rose would not be denied its place in the new world
where it was already blooming when they arrived. The importance of the
Rose family (*Rosaceae*) in producing food for the world and in the development of our culture is second only to that of the grass or grain family. And
if this seems surprising, think of the history of this prolific Mother Hubbard
of the plant family to which we owe so much.

Botanists believe that the rose was one of the very earliest flowers to
develop in the primitive springtime of the world. Over stretches of millions
of years, by subtle changes the rose adapted itself to many varieties of climate
and location, finally becoming hardy, disease-resistant, fragrant, and beautiful.
It also produced many offspring of varying character which became fruits,
such as the strawberry, raspberry, blackberry, thimbleberry, dewberry. Shrubby
roses grew, some of which became the steeplebush of New England pastures,
cotoneasters, flowering quince, flowering almond. Some grew into trees which
became pear, apple, peach, quince, apricot, shadbush, cherry, mountain ash,
plum, and hawthorn.

However varied in form were their individual characteristics, these scattered members of the *Rosaceae* nevertheless had special features in common
which brought them into the Rose family. Sometimes it was the number of
petals, usually five; or the thorns; or the numerous stamens; or the manner
in which the fruits were formed. The first member of the Rose family to get
publicity was that famous apple tree "in the beginning." But the rose in one
of its many forms has preceded or followed man around wherever he has

gone. Some bit of the family—in applesauce and dehydrated strawberries—even went to the moon on man's first landing there.

Although most of them bloom only once a year, in June, the old-fashioned roses of early American gardens are still the most reliable, the most fragrant, and, to many, the most charming of all. Dooryard gardens scattered across New England harbor many old varieties such as the beloved Cinnamon rose (its leaves when crushed have a faint fragrance of cinnamon), a small, double-pink, sweetly scented rose. The native swamp or pasture roses may often be found in country gardens. The old Cabbage roses always found in Victorian gardens are still beloved by many. This rose was often pictured in Currier and Ives prints, thereby hanging on many a cottage wall in addition to being in the garden. The Moss roses have delicious fragrance and charming flowers, so popular that they were once considered "common." They inspired designs on the plates and cups of Victorian tea tables. The Maiden's Blush has the sweetest of all fragrances, the daintiest of petals flushed with pale pink, and rich abundant foliage of a handsome blue-green color. Many of the Gallica and Damask roses can still be found growing wild in old dooryards or cemeteries, reminiscent of the cottage gardens where they once flourished. These, along with the Rugosas of the seaside and the Spinosissima (Scottish), are among the hardiest of roses for northern gardens.

Oh, a garden containing only old-fashioned roses would be a dream garden of unexcelled charm, fragrance, and beauty.

New England housewives made the most of their roses. They made rosewater for flavoring cakes, frostings, and beverages—and for bathing, so refreshing on a hot day. They used the petals in sachets and potpourris; candied petals* for cake decorations; made jam and jelly and tea and wine, love potions, beauty salves, and perfumes. Rose petals were added to snuff. Many of the receipts for roses have been handed down through the generations and are still in use today.

* See my New England Butt'ry Shelf Cookbook, page 24.

As roses were found in every old garden, so were herbs of many kinds and uses. At first they were planted for medicinal purposes. Every neighborhood was graced by housewives who were well versed in the use of those "simples." Those who used them did not really know why the herbs provided healing and balm, but their faculties were so appreciated that the first medical books, the herbals, were written to identify herbs and delineate their uses. From the beginning in America, women collected from the woods and fields and their own gardens such simples or common herbs as could be used to relieve or cure the family or village ills.

Some of the herbs of our gardens have had a fanciful past, having been not only the medicine of olden times, but superstitiously thought to have had mysterious powers of witchcraft. More importantly, herbs have been used for cooking, either as potherbs or as flavoring for food. And herbs have had other uses.

Many years ago it was the custom to carry a "Sunday posy" to church, a pretty flower the stem of which was discreetly wrapped in a handkerchief within which was also concealed a sprig of fragrant herbs. Churchgoers spent the long hours of the sermon and prayers smelling their Sunday posies. The concealed sprig of southernwood (which was called "meetin' plant") or fennel or costmary kept them awake, gave them something pleasant to do, and helped to pass dragging hours. It might even have produced some happy daydreaming.

Young people carried "meetin' seeds" to nibble in church. Fennel, dill, or caraway seeds were thought to stay the hiccoughs, but it was also known that nibbling these sharp-tasting seeds discouraged drowsiness and sleeping, surely a common complaint during a three-hour Sunday discourse.

Nosegays or "tussy-mussies" made from flowers mingled with sweet-scented herbs were given to favorite friends. Herb teas were made, as we have seen, by the country people, and by the good wives of ardent patriots during the American Revolution. The now-familiar roadside herb tansy was hung in doorways to discourage gnats and flies, or rubbed on kitchen tables to prevent ants. Lavender and rosemary sprigs were cut and laid in chests containing clothing or linens to freshen them and discourage destructive moths. Herbs have been used in the manufacture of toiletries.

Happily, there has been a resurgence of interest in herbs, not only in medicine and cooking, but as garden plants. They are again cherished for their special virtues of fragrance and taste and beauty. It has been rediscovered that herbs are useful, and more than that, they have charm and are fun to grow and use.

Harvesting of herbs begins in June. Cut the first sage for drying; and the lavender just before the blossoms open. Cut angelica stems in June and candy them for decorating cakes and cookies, as has been done for centuries in the old countries of Europe as well as in America. And—

> Gather thee rosebuds while ye may
> Old time is still a-flying
> And that same flower that smiles today
> Tomorrow will be dying.
>
> —ROBERT HERRICK

CANDIED ANGELICA

Cut young tender stems of angelica, wash and dry. With a sharp knife, cut diagonal slices about ¾ inch long. Simmer the pieces in water until tender. This may take an hour or even 2 hours, but it is important that they be tender.

When tender, drain thoroughly. In a saucepan, make a thick syrup by boiling together 1 cup of water and 3 cups of sugar. Add green coloring. Immerse the angelica pieces and simmer until they look translucent. Remove from heat, place angelica pieces in sterilized jam jar, pour hot syrup over, and seal.

When ready to use for decorating cakes, remove pieces from jar one at a time and cut to form leaves or stems. Jar may then be kept indefinitely in icebox for further use.

CRYSTALLIZED ANGELICA

Follow above directions, but do not put in jar. Instead, when boiling the angelica pieces in the thick syrup, boil it down until the pieces have absorbed all of the syrup, stirring frequently to prevent sticking or burning. Then remove from fire and spread pieces on a buttered cooky pan. When cool, sift granulated sugar generously over the pieces, turning with spatula so that all sides of all pieces are thoroughly sugared. Leave overnight to dry thoroughly, then pack lightly into airtight jars or boxes.

ROSEWATER

Collect a pound of scented rose petals and put them in a heatproof glass, enamel, or pottery pan on the fire. Cover petals with water and bring to a boil, then simmer gently for 10 minutes. Strain off the water. May be used for bathing the face and arms on a warm day—very refreshing. It is best bottled and kept ice cold in the refrigerator.

ROSE PETAL MARMALADE

4 quarts gently packed, clean, unsprayed rose petals	⅓ cup fresh lemon juice
2 quarts boiling water	red food coloring (if roses are pale in color)
8 cups sugar	

Place the rose petals in a large enamel preserving kettle and pour the boiling water over them. With wooden spoon, push the petals gently down into the water, then cover the kettle and let the petals steep for 20 minutes.

With a skimmer or slotted spoon, remove petals, squeezing all possible juice out of them into kettle. Reserve the petals.

To the liquid remaining in the kettle, add the sugar and lemon juice. Bring to a full rolling boil and cook until jelly stage is reached (220° on jelly thermometer, or until the syrup sheets when dropped from the side of a metal spoon). Skim off the froth.

Add the petals to the jelly (and some coloring if desired at this point to make pink jelly). Stir to separate the petals and mix them with the jelly. Start testing immediately and when the liquid again reaches jelly stage, remove pan from heat. Let the marmalade stand in the kettle for 10 minutes, stir well again and pour with a ladle into hot sterilized jam jars. With a damp cloth wipe off any drips of jam from the edge of jars, then cover jam with a layer of melted paraffin. Cover jars when cool; store in cool dry place.

This is a delicious confection for hot scones or biscuits or thin-sliced homemade bread at tea time.

SAVORY HERB BUTTER

Soften a stick of butter (¼ lb.) to room temperature. Chop well 1 Tbs. parsley or rosemary, thyme, marjoram, dill, basil, or chives, or a combination of some of those herbs, and mix well with the butter. (Or use the contents of a "Chef's Delight Soup Bag" from the Greene Herb Gardens, Greene, R.I.)

Put a teaspoonful of Herb Butter on baked fish when serving it at table. Put it in green beans, broiled tomatoes, on steak, oven-baked or fried chicken, lamb chops, meat loaf, or hamburger.

Use the chive butter for baked potato or boiled potatoes; parsley butter for potatoes or fish. Use the dill or rosemary butter for hot biscuits.

Use the basil butter to top a tureenful of hot tomato soup.

Use the thyme butter to top a platter of scrambled eggs.

Fresh chopped herbs can be folded into little envelopes of wax paper and frozen for use in the winter.

Herbs when chopped and dried can be tied into small squares of cheese-cloth to make *bouquet garni* for use in soups, stews, stock, and gravies; also in salads.

> Here's flowers for you:
> Hot lavender, mints, savory, marjoram;
> And marigold that goes to bed wi' the sun
> And with him rises weeping.
>
> —WILLIAM SHAKESPEARE

Portrait—The Greene Herb Gardens

A CHEF'S DELIGHT

THERE were people milling all around. Everyone was carrying something. The buzz of talking and laughing under the trees was like the busy excitement of swarming bees. Some people seemed to be tasting or chewing and a voice said, "I haven't had horehound candy since I was a youngster." Another voice from another direction said heartily, "Oh, I only dip candles as a hobby really; I'm a minister of the Gospel." Two ladies elegantly dressed in nineteenth-century costume were autographing books as fast as their gloved hands would permit. Another lady was standing on a hillside looking into a wave of faces below her and saying emphatically, "Now, let's eat right and be lovely." A tweed-jacketed man was wandering off under the apple trees walking a corgi named Steddy, and another was coming out of the greenhouse with a healthy tarragon plant in a large clay pot saying, "A chef's delight, a *real* chef's delight." Two women seemed particularly busy greeting and shaking hands and answering questions. One was shy, gentle, in a trim suit with a brimmed hat shading her eyes; the other hearty, suntanned, wearing slacks and a worn suede jacket. Yes, there were people milling all around, and everyone was carrying something.

The occasion was a garden party at the Greene Herb Gardens in the high rolling hills of western Rhode Island, near the Connecticut line. It was not exactly a social event, although the best people were there. It was a benefit for a local garden club and it had attracted—as it does each year—people from all the New England states and even New York, who came to see, to buy, to participate, to enjoy.

The Greene Herb Gardens are situated on the large, well-kept estate of one of Rhode Island's oldest families, and they are famous all over the country wherever people live who are interested in growing things, especially herbs. The Gardens consist of the large main house, with a small aromatic shop located across the carriage drive where the dried herbs which are the product of the Gardens are on display for sale; a greenhouse, drying shed, various other outbuildings, a number of acres of growing plants, and several delightful knot herb gardens which are a joy to wander in any day of the growing year, even in the rain, when the dampness seems to release the fragrance of the plants.

The Greene Herb Gardens were established in 1942 by Miss Mittie Arnold and Miss Margaret Thomas. They had found a mutual interest and challenge in growing and using herbs and decided to pursue it as a business. Miss Arnold's own home was a perfect site with its quiet location in the hills, surrounded by stone walls, great trees, farms, and fields. The village of Greene nearby would scarcely be noticed if one were driving through it; but it is on the map mostly because of its small but famous industry, the Herb Gardens, a mile or two beyond the little church.

In the beginning, the enterprise was a struggle. Neither of the ladies was an expert on herbs, and they devoted long hours to study. Neither of them was afraid of work and they pitched in with all the help they could find, to till the fields, plant the seeds, transplant, weed, harvest, dry, and process the herbs. They spent as much time on their hands and knees in the gardens as their help did, until they became organized and had perfected their own systems of doing the chores.

In those days, much of their help came from the village, and included school-age boys who worked during the summer. We know of two brothers who applied for summer jobs at the Gardens. They were interviewed by Miss Thomas, who asked them a few questions, and then she said, "John, do you smoke?" "No, ma'am," replied John. "Bradford, do you smoke?" "Yes, ma'am, sometimes," replied Bradford. "All right," replied Miss Thomas. "We will pay John ten cents an hour more than Bradford, and if you will follow me, I will show you what your job for today will be."

Help is getting increasingly difficult to get these days, and is decreasingly willing to learn, according to Miss Arnold. "They all know more than we do," she said. "We had a full-time gardener a few years ago who was asked to harvest the marjoram. Margaret watched him for a few minutes, then suggested that he was cutting it too low. 'I know what I'm doing,' he said, and went on cutting as he wished. As a result, we lost our whole marjoram planting that year."

Not long ago, Miss Arnold and Miss Thomas paid us an afternoon call, and we had a most enjoyable chat about the Gardens and what they had meant to the two ladies. "Our real interest all these years," Miss Thomas said, "has been seeing this thing which we love—the growing and use of herbs—take hold of other people. We have done our best to encourage this interest by dispensing seeds, plants, plans for gardens and uses of herbs, and other information. It is so much better for a housewife to go out of her own kitchen door and pick off snippets of the fresh herbs she needs than it is to buy them packaged at the supermarket—who knows how long they have been on the shelf?"

That their encouragement has taken effect is plain to be seen in the now-widespread interest in herbs, in the amount of business they do, and in the bundles of mail they receive from all over the world.

Their biggest interest is in the field of culinary herbs. In the field of herbs for medicine, the present-day pharmacy and laboratory have taken over from the housewife of old who picked and dispensed her "simples" from the kitchen door—except for the country people. In some sections of New England and the South, herbs are still widely used for medicine. A great deal of research is still being done in pharmacy to determine what medicinal qualities the various herbs do contain.

"I have a large interesting file of letters from country people all over, which has told me so much about the uses they make of herbs," said Miss Thomas. "We cannot—nor do we wish to—dispense advice on using herbs for medicine, but we certainly find it an interesting part of our work to learn what others consider remedies for various illnesses. For instance, we have shipped great quantities of the roots of a certain herb to a man in British Columbia, who claimed he used it as a cancer cure."

Miss Arnold looked thoughtful. "People who are one or two generations removed from European backgrounds make much more use of herbs for the kitchen as well as medicinal purposes than most Americans do," she said. "There was a group of ladies who came out from a Greek church in the city one day," she added with a gentle laugh. "We came to a little plot of land that we hadn't got around to cultivating yet but which was going to be planted soon. One of the ladies spied the pigweed with which the ground there was covered. They *dove* into it and pulled up the whole patch—we got cartons for them to put it all into and our cultivating was all done for us! In Europe they had used pigweed as a vegetable. One lady said she cooked it with potatoes. They had the *best* time." Miss Thomas added that Italians love to come to the Gardens to gather mallow, which they use as a green and also for tea. "We just consider it mostly as a weed in this country, like the pigweed," she said.

In curiosity I asked, "What have been your best sellers?"

"Sage, of course; but for a long time our blended poultry seasoning was used at the original Pepperidge Farm in Norwalk, Connecticut, and we consequently sold more of that than anything else," Miss Thomas answered. It seems that during the Second World War, Mrs. Rudkin, owner of Pepperidge Farm, was unable to get the sage she required from Europe, and was about to give up marketing poultry dressing when she discovered the Greene Herb Gardens.

"She said she had to have the *very best* for her products," Miss Arnold emphasized. "And so we supplied her for many years. Finally she asked us for the recipe. We gave it to her in a burst of Margaret's generosity," she continued, looking at her partner with mild reproach. "So far as we know the recipe is still used for the poultry dressing now marketed by the company which bought Pepperidge Farm and its products."

"Tell me what has been your greatest pleasure over the years in your work with herbs," I said, and Miss Arnold was quick in her reply. "Well, I just love herbs, and have loved working with them, learning about them, seeing them grow. I can't ever throw away an herb plant, I love every little plant."

"Yes, Mittie is the botanist," said Margaret. "She is also a born collector. If there is a new plant, Mittie will know about it. Each plant talks to her, and she treats each one as an individual. For myself, I enjoy the people that come and go, whether they come to us out of curiosity, or botanical interest in the plants, or because they want to make use of herbs, or just to breathe the clean air of the country. I have also loved the Gardens because of the closeness of our work to the really basic important things of life—the sunshine and fresh air, the good earth and growing things." They both looked thoughtful and rather pleased with their thoughts. Their hands were work-hardened and their faces were sun- and wind-worn; their expressions contented and happy.

Although time was valuable to our guests, we all found it difficult to break away, and so we talked of some of the projects Miss Arnold and Miss Thomas had participated in during their years in business. They told of supplying shops everywhere with herb seeds and products. Their special *bouquet garni* known as "Chef's Delight" is sold at the Cathedral Herb Shop in Washington, D.C., as it is in many other places in the country. They supply many gift and herb shops with dried herbs, and told of one important dealer who sold so much of their products that he asked them to come in each week to fill his shelves. "My goodness, we don't have time to do *that!"* said Miss Mittie. However, Miss Thomas somehow finds time to talk of herbs in a radio broadcast once each week and she has many devoted listeners.

They take pride in having helped Old Sturbridge Village lay out the early-nineteenth-century herb garden which is so well displayed at the restoration village in Massachusetts. "Even today we supply them with the seeds which they plant in their herb garden," Miss Arnold said. "They are the *very best* seeds and products that can be found, and that's why Old Sturbridge Village uses them."

The interesting Dye Garden which has been established at the old Slater Mill restoration in Pawtucket, Rhode Island, was partially supplied from Greene Herb Gardens. This garden displays plants which were used for purposes of dyeing yarns for weaving. "This year we are again helping the Herb Society of America do a unique herb garden for the Slater Mill project," Miss Thomas said. "And gardens for the blind—well, my goodness—we were instrumental in establishing a real interest in such gardens. Years ago two ladies visited our display at the Boston Flower Show. We talked with them and the subject of the blind came up. We idly mused a bit by saying that such and such an herb would be a lovely plant for the blind to enjoy. It turned out that the visitors were interested in the Perkins Institute for the Blind. Then we all became so interested in the idea of a garden for the blind that the ladies joined the Herb Society of America, in which we have always been so active, and we eventually exhibited a garden for the blind at the Boston Flower Show—a garden for taste and smell and touch. We also have helped work out the delightful garden located at the Bureau for the Blind on Broad Street, Providence. We know that garden clubs all over the country now are working on special herb gardens for the blind, and we are proud to have had a part in getting this interest established."

Dreaming of many new projects ahead, Miss Arnold and Miss Thomas speak of their files which are well stocked with their own receipts for the use of herbs in cooking and with letters from interesting customers all over the world. Their memories are rich in experiences which symbolize the fulfillment of their "real interest" in herbs—that of spreading the word to gardeners everywhere on the joys of growing and using herbs. Without moving from their perfect New England setting, two delightful, modest ladies touch the lives of many people in a most unusual way.

The Lady's Almanac for 1856 told the story of a young bride who received as a wedding gift a shipment containing twenty fruit trees for planting in her new orchard. She decided to plant them in rows of five trees in a row. Unfortunately, one of the young trees was dead. But she still planted her nineteen remaining trees, five in a row as she wished, making nine rows. Can you solve her problem of making such a planting? You will find the answer elsewhere in the *Butt'ry Shelf Almanac.* Watch for it.

JULY

Birthstone and Birthdays

July's Birthstone is the *Ruby*, for *Friendship*.

1	16
2	17
3	18
4	19
5	20
6	21
7	22
8	23
9	24
10	25
11	26
12	27
13	28
14	29
15	30
	31

Flower

THE LILY
Lilium

THE Lily has been known over the centuries as a flower which symbolized Purity because of the whiteness of the parent flower of this very large and ancient family. *Liliaceae* is one of the really basic prehistoric flower families from which have sprung many colors and many kinds of flowers. Men and gods for ages past have been concerned with the Lily and its mythical, magical, and medicinal powers.

Today there are myriad lilies which have sprung naturally or been hybridized from the first lilies of the world. Members of the family grow in a wide area. In New England several lilies are native, including the *Lilium Philadelphicum* which is also called Philadelphia Lily, Red Lily, or Wood Lily; the *Lilium Canadense*, or Canada Lily or Yellow Lily; the *Lilium superbum*, or Turk's-cap Lily; the various Trilliums; the *Erythronium* which is also called Trout Lily, Adder's Tongue, or Dog's-tooth Violet; and the delicate *Aletris farinosa*, or Star Grass. The Tawny Lily which one sees along roadsides all over New England is not a native but an escapee from colonial gardens into the fields and roadsides.

Other familiar members of the Lily family are onions, asparagus, lily-of-the-valley, hyacinths, daylilies, squill, and Star-of-Bethlehem. Most lilies found in flower gardens today have been imported and hybridized. They are of easy culture as potted or hardy garden plants, depending upon their species, and they lend a stately dignity and beauty to gardens. It is possible to have some member of the Lily family in bloom in the garden from earliest spring to fall in a wide range of colors.

To gild refined gold, to paint the lily,
To throw a perfume on the violet,
To smooth the ice, or add another hue
Unto the rainbow, or with taper-light
To seek the beauteous eye of heaven to garnish
Is wasteful and ridiculous excess.

—WILLIAM SHAKESPEARE

Bird

THE BOBOLINK
Dolichonyx oryzivorus

A VERY OLD book on birds gives a translation of the Bobolink's song made by one to whom the happy free song of this bird was meaningful:

> Liberty liberty
> Nice to be free!
> Bobolink where he please,
> Fly in de apple-trees;
> Oh 'tis the freedom note
> Guggle sweet in his throat.
> Jink-a-link, jink-a-jink,
> Winky wink, winky wink,
> Only tink, only tink,
> How happy, Bobolink!
> Sweet! Sweet!

It is perhaps as good a translation as could possibly be made of the bubbling, mirthful, merry song of this gay bird. The Bobolink sings from the top of a tree, from a fencepost or stone wall, from the swaying stalk of a mullein or milkweed, and he sings most joyously when flying through the air over the fields he inhabits.

Traveling five thousand or so miles from the northern part of Argentina, he arrives in New England in May or June and we are always sure of his arrival date, for he immediately breaks into ecstatic song from the top of the butternut tree. When the East Field is bright with grass and flowers, he comes to home-stake in the sunlight there. He lives where the sweet-smelling hay, the violet, the daisy and clover, the buttercup and wild straw-berry, the black-eyed susans and goldenrod grow.

He builds his loose cup of a nest out of grass and plant stems deep in the midst of the sunny meadows or along the grassy margins of marshes. He can often be seen in such places, swaying back and forth in the breeze perched on a firm stalk of weed, and very often he will be singing deliriously as he sits there clowning and performing like the harlequin of the summer-time that he is.

The Bobolink is a handsome, dashing bird who wears a costume of black elegantly trimmed in yellow, buff, and white. His wife is a demurely dressed lady of softer color, yellow-brown dashed with dark streaks.

Bobolinks are rather late in nesting; usually there is one nesting of five to seven bluish-white eggs spotted with brown. Their late nesting is often their undoing, for if hay fields where they live are cut before the middle of July, their nests are destroyed for the year. They feast splendidly on the insects of the field: grasshoppers, crickets, beetles, spiders. But in the autumn they resort to seeds and grain and are often seen in large flocks in the rice fields of the south when they migrate.

This gay bird goes by many names—Maybird, Meadowbird, and Butter-bird among them. There is no end of song and dance while he lives in New England, for he constantly frolics while singing, perched or in flight over the fields. He is a clown on the wing. The song is long and strong, begin-ning easily, with a gradual crescendo of such rapidity and bubbling merriness that it sometimes seems as if a dozen birds were singing at once.

His nest is very difficult to find, and although we have known of many nestings, we have found only one. When an early cutting of hay in the East Field was necessary, we have tried to locate the nests so that they could be left undisturbed by the mower, but this has been impossible. It no longer matters whether the hay is cut so early, so the little families are now safe.

The Bobolink has a way of alighting in the field a long way from his nest, and then scooting through the grass at ground level to avoid detection of the nest. When alarmed, he utters a *chuck*, flying nervously from one perch to another, spreading his tail in his expression of concern.

The nature writer Edwin Way Teale described the Bobolink song as being a jingling song, and wondered if we could say a jingle of Bobolinks as we say a gaggle of geese, an exaltation of larks, a waddling of ducks. It is more than a jingle, it is a bubbling like fizzy champagne, so perhaps we could say a bubble of Bobolinks. It is also a peal of gay merry laughter, a delirious melody which tumbles out faster and faster until the end of the song—and then begins again.

At the end of the summer, the male Bobolink casts off his elegant dress-coat, assumes the quieter color of his mate, and stops his singing. The birds leave without fanfare for the long journey to Argentina and we miss their happy presence on the farm.

William Cullen Bryant's eight-versed poem called "Robert of Lincoln" tells in delightful verse the saga of the Bobolink which we in our family learned by heart as children. Often as we hear the gay lilting song of our own "Robert of Lincoln" we repeat some of its accurately descriptive lines.

Merrily swinging on brier and weed,
   Near to the nest of his little dame,
Over the mountain-side or mead,
   Robert of Lincoln is telling his name:
     "Bob-o'-link, bob-o'-link,
     Spink, spank, spink;
Snug and safe is that nest of ours,
Hidden among the summer flowers.
     Chee, chee, chee."

Tug at the Bell Rope

Through the open door
A drowsy smell of flowers—gray heliotrope,
And white sweet clover, and shy mignonette—
Comes faintly in, and silent chorus lends
To the pervading symphony of peace.
                                        —JOHN GREENLEAF WHITTIER

LIKE a little sailboat in the harbor at eventide, we are becalmed in July. Even the birds seem quieter; all through the day there are periods of deep quiet, a "pervading symphony of peace." We seek the coolest corners, the easiest tasks. From the fields wafts the scent of new-mown hay, and from somewhere in the distance drifts the sound of the mowers. How beautifully quiet it must have been when mowing was done by hand. Only the rhythmic whetting of the scythes disturbed the midsummer air then. Now the scythe is used only for trimming, and few know the skill, the grace, and the beauty of mowing by hand.

There was a storied man who lived in our town who could mow by hand six acres a day, giving nine tons of hay; his strong, long arms cut a swath twelve feet wide. This man had other early New England capabilities, for during his lifetime he made by hand and sold one million shingles. He had cleared three hundred acres of land for his farm, tapped for twenty years at least six hundred maple trees, and made as much as four thousand pounds of sugar a year. In his spare time he worked as a cooper and he was a famous drum-maker as well. Where could be found such industry in a man now?

CLAMBAKE IN A KETTLE

There is a haze over the mountain which brings it very close. Flies are biting, the swallows fly low, and a thunderstorm could be on its way. Mr. Shaw, who brings us eggs, stops by and as he scans the sky says, "Don't like the look of the clouds. If it rains on a Monday we won't have no week for hayin'."

I take a walk through the garden, picking off a few dead blossoms, pulling a few weeds, tying an occasional delphinium or lily. As I approach the herb garden, the air is laden with the scent of rosemary and mint and thyme and the "shy mignonette."

July is rich in flowers as the annuals and biennials begin to bloom. They fill the borders with color and fragrance for many weeks to come. In country gardens and town gardens alike, the hollyhocks, petunias, nasturtiums, verbena, cosmos, zinnias, and marigolds bloom abundantly and with riotous colors, asking only occasional watering during dry spells.

In the woods, foliage is dense, dark, and cool. Leafage on bush and tree is full grown. In the fields and roadsides still unmown, the daisies, red clover, buttercups, and paintbrush catch the sun in vivid color and dancing light.

There are anxious notes and excited calls from songbirds worried about their fledglings, now so susceptible to cat and crow and hawk and snake. I worry, too. We watch the bluebirds teaching their young to bathe. Cherries are ripe, and the robins and cedar waxwings take over in the loaded boughs of the old trees. A bobolink sings in the butternut tree. Our wild strawberries are ripe, and later the black-cap raspberries will be gathered in an old Shaker basket. The first blueberries ripen; they are poured into a blue bowl to be eaten with thick cream.

It seems such a good time to do nothing—until someone suggests that wild strawberries are most appropriately used if they are scattered atop a great dishful of homemade vanilla ice cream. Ice and salt are readied, rich creamy custard stirred, and soon both ice cream and strawberries have vanished along with the laziness.

On the Fourth of July, we tug at the bell rope in the barn and put up the flag to wave in the hot breeze, remembering that after John Adams signed the Declaration of Independence on the first American Fourth of July, he wrote his wife Abigail that he hoped Americans would always make this day one of rejoicing and merrymaking. We follow his wishes willingly.

Radishes, lettuce, tiny carrots, and beet greens are gathered from the vegetable garden; new peas are shelled and new potatoes scrubbed to go with the whole salmon for the traditional New England July Fourth dinner, a very special occasion indeed.

On the village greens in New England in July there are many activities beginning with the Fourth celebrations. Summer theaters and music festivals listed in the Sunday summer entertainment supplements of metropolitan newspapers are well attended, as are the dance festivals and art exhibits. Auctions these days are getting sophisticated, attended by collectors of rare and not-so-rare Americana who are willing to pay high prices. Hidden down the country lanes of some old towns, however, an occasional good country auction can still be found where a prized piece of Sandwich glass or an old bottle or a fine tool may still be had at a respectable price along with the broken-down mail-order chairs, leaky saucepans, and musty books.

Village fairs are often gay and rewarding, their colorful booths stocked with homemade and home-grown goodies from apple pies to zinnias; with hand-stitched, crocheted, woven, and embroidered articles from aprons to zebras (stuffed toy zebras, of course).

The first fair of this kind in New England (it is still called *"the* Fair" by some Bostonians) was organized by Sarah Josepha Hale to raise the funds needed for completion of the Bunker Hill Monument. For months ladies all over New England and as far away as Ohio sewed, crocheted, cross-stitched, quilted, knit, made jelly and pickles and sent them to Quincy Hall in Boston where the great fair was held. It lasted for seven days and drew crowds of people. Elaborate booths and decorations made a display such as had never before been seen in America. It was such a success that it has been the inspiration for similar fund-raising events all over the country in the century and a half since it was held.

There are barbecues and strawberry festivals, open-house tours and flower shows, band concerts and fish fries. And there are flea markets.

The flea markets of New England are relatively new. It is thought that they first appeared in Connecticut, started by an enterprising young man with a wide hay field at his disposal. He devised a plan wherein he persuaded some antique dealers to fill their station wagons with wares and come to his field for a day. He marked off places for them to park in rows, advertised for customers who came in droves, and the first New England flea market was a success. The idea spread quickly. It is now a way of making money for churches, historical societies, restoration projects, scholarship funds—and of course it makes some money for the participants unless the day happens to be a stormy one.

On the common of many of even the smallest towns and villages, there will occasionally be held in summer a fair or a flea market of small pretension and large diversity of wares. In our own village the Historical Society organizes the flea market and does the advertising. The "dealers" participating are not usually bona fide merchants, but may be housewives, schoolteachers, farmers, amateur coin or stamp collectors, retired businessmen or women, all with something to sell or exchange which is not necessarily antique. Lunch is usually served by the church Ladies' Aid or the Grange. The "Friends of the Library" have a display of old books for sale at ten cents each. Customers go away with armloads of them, good for summer reading, good for collecting, good bargains all. We bought a 1910 leatherbound unabridged dictionary in fine condition priced at ten cents; then spent months finding an old-fashioned wrought-iron dictionary stand to hold it. Profusely illustrated with delightful drawings, the big old book is a most imposing piece of equipment in our home library, dwarfing the modern dictionaries in interest and size if not importance.

Part of the fun of such a flea market is finding out what prompts the sellers to participate. The wife of a professional man explains, "I love antiques and enjoy buying them, but when I get more than I have room for I have to get rid of them. By displaying at the flea markets now and then, I can trade something I no longer want for something I like better." A retired businessman from the city said, "It gives my wife and me something to do besides just sitting around at home watching the television." A farmer's wife said, "We had so many old things in the attic that I thought I might as well help pay taxes by selling them—our taxes are dreadful, you know, all these new elaborate schools—and I have the fun of seeing a lot of people besides." Demonstrating rug-braiding, a young woman sells a few rugs, earning enough money to pay for the rugs she makes for her own home. "My hobby *has* to pay for itself," she says simply. A young boy arranges a table full of bottles. He talks very knowledgeably with his customers about his bottles, which he has dug from old dumps. At the end of the day his eyes are alight with excitement.

The Historical Society adds enough to its treasury to pay for needed improvements in its headquarters and provides a profitable and pleasant day for many.

Some of these fête days are to be found in other parts of the country as well as New England, but nowhere else in the world is there to be found a real New England clambake. A fine clambake can be held anywhere along a seashore, or even in one's own backyard if one is willing to forswear certain of the amenities of the Cape Cod or Rhode Island bakes, such as being in New England and tasting the New England salt sea air.

A New England clambake is in a way a man's affair. Presided over, planned, produced, and cooked by men, it is nevertheless also enjoyed by women and children. The clambake was a favorite feast of the Indians long before Englishmen landed on these shores. Along the northeast coast where clams were plentiful in the clean sand, Indians held tribal bakes in which the methods used for cooking the ingredients were little different from the ones in use today.

The Fourth of July signals the start of the clambake season in Rhode Island, at the beach or in a Rhode Island pasture or backyard. The really big ones are well organized and are directed by a bakemaster who may have held his post for many years, experience being considered one of the necessary qualifications for a proper master. At one bake we know, even the helpers and waiters attend their traditional duties year after year, earning their places in the clambake hierarchy by diligent work and loyal attention to duties.

It is traditional to serve New England Clam Chowder first, rich and delicious. It would be considered a disgrace if there were any hint of tomato in this chowder. With the chowder is served deep-fat-fried clam cakes (or fritters) and pilot crackers.

The Indians prepared their bake on the sand, and in some bakes this is still done. Others prepare a pit, into which white-hot rocks are pushed, rock-weed (seaweed) and the ingredients of the bake are added, then more rockweed on top. The whole is covered with heavy canvas and allowed to steam for forty-five minutes or more until all the ingredients are tender and well cooked. Smaller bakes can be done in a barrel, or even on the kitchen stove.

A small calico-covered cookbook called *A Rhode Island Rule Book* was compiled by Mrs. Leah Lapham from an old family book of "rules" for cooking which dated back to the early 1800's. In this delightful book Mrs. Lapham gave a very good receipt for chowder according to old Rhode Island custom.

NEW ENGLAND CLAM CHOWDER

Fry 4 slices of minced salt pork until brown; add 2 sliced onions and fry. Remove pork and onion from pork fat and add to fat 4 cups water, 4 cups diced potato. Cook until potatoes are nearly done then add 4 cups of chopped clams from which all black parts have been removed. Salt and pepper to taste.

Scald 3 cups rich milk, add to first mixture. Let it come to a boil and pour into hot tureen in which 4 pilot (or other) crackers have been broken, together with an eighth of a pound of butter.

This traditional chowder serves 6 people.

> The chowder on the sand beach made
> Dipped by the hungry, steaming hot,
> With spoons of clam-shells from the pot.
> —JOHN GREENLEAF WHITTIER

CLAM FRITTERS

Remove all black parts from a pint of shucked clams and chop clams fine. Add 2 beaten eggs, ¼ tsp. black pepper, 1 tsp. salt, 1 cup rich milk, and 1 Tbs. finely chopped or grated onion. Sift together 1¾ cups flour and 1 Tbs. baking powder. Add the clam mixture to flour mixture and stir together until well blended.

With a teaspoon, drop the batter into deep hot fat (375°) and fry until nicely browned. Drain on paper towels. This will serve 4 to 6 persons.

RHODE ISLAND SHORE CLAMBAKE
IN A BARREL WITH LOBSTERS

For each person to be served, have ready the following:

1 live lobster (1–1½ lbs.)	2 or 3 ears of fresh corn, silks
12 scrubbed and rinsed fresh	and outer husks removed
clams in the shell	2 small new potatoes in jackets
	2 small peeled onions

Other additions may be sweet potatoes, sausages, servings of bluefish or haddock wrapped in heavy paper.

Put potatoes and onions into a cheesecloth or net bag for convenience in handling.

Have ready a bushel basket of fresh clean rockweed (seaweed) and a pail of clean sea water.

Gather driftwood and build a good hot fire. Place on the fire enough rocks the size of cobblestones or larger to fill the barrel about one-third full. Heat the rocks on the fire for a couple of hours until they are white hot.

Meanwhile, dig a hole in the sand which is deep enough to sink the barrel about two-thirds or more of its depth. When the rocks are ready, throw sea water into the barrel to wet the sides and bottom, put in a thick layer of seaweed, then put in the hot rocks, using heavy tongs or heatproof gloves for handling them.

Put more seaweed on top of the rocks. Add the clams and lobster, another layer of seaweed. Add potatoes and onions in their bag, then a layer of corn and other additions as suggested. Top all with a thick layer of seaweed, pour in a quart or two of sea water. Cover the top and exposed sides of the barrel with a heavy canvas and scoop sand around and over the top to cover securely.

Let the bake steam for an hour or more, then remove sand, canvas, and seaweed; serve the food with tongs.

Have ready melted butter, crisp cucumbers, onions, sliced tomatoes, and vinegar or lemon wedges. For dessert, serve pieces of ice-cold watermelon.

One bit of advice: prepare this bake inshore from the high tide line.

CLAMBAKE IN A KETTLE

A large enamel kettle is excellent for this bake, which may be prepared on the kitchen stove and serves 4 people.

Scrub and rinse 4 quarts of fresh clams in the shell.

Cut into 4 portions about 1 lb. bluefish, haddock, or mackerel and put each portion into a separate small paper bag.

Peel 4 small onions. Scrub well 4 carrots, 4 white potatoes, and 4 sweet potatoes. Remove outside layer of husks, and remove all silks from 4 ears of sweet corn.

Have ready 1 lb. link sausages and 4 1-lb. or chicken lobsters.

Into the bottom of the kettle put a layer of fresh seaweed if possible. Then put in the clams, onions, carrots, potatoes, sausages, fish, corn, and lobsters in that order. Over this pour 2 or 3 cups of clean sea water if possible; or cold well or tap water. (If the kettle seems just too full, dip the ears of corn-in-the-husks in water and place in the oven at 350° for 30 minutes.)

Cover the kettle, put on high heat until it starts to steam, then turn down the fire and cook for 45 minutes. Serve nicely arranged on a large platter, removing paper bags from the fish before placing on the platter.

Strain out the broth from the kettle and serve in hot cups.

In a cookbook titled *The Good Housekeeper, or The Way to Live Well,* which was published in Boston in 1835 by Sarah Josepha Hale, there is a receipt for a beverage which would be appropriate to go with a traditional clambake. We have not tested this receipt. The title page of the cookbook, which contained practical rules for cooking, bears the quotation, "Temperate in all things.—Bible."

"COMMON BEER"

"Two gallons of water to a large handful of hops is the rule. A little fresh gathered spruce, or sweet fern makes the beer more agreeable, and you may allow a quart of wheat bran to the mixture—then boil it two or three hours. Strain it through a sieve, and stir in, while the liquor is hot, a teacup of molasses to every gallon. Let it stand till lukewarm, pour it into a clean barrel and add good yeast, a pint if the barrel is nearly full; shake it well together; it will be fit for use the next day.

"Fermented liquors, if used at all as a drink, should be very sparingly taken."

Devote your search for these alone:
The sand that's salted by the sea,
The driftwood fire, the rounded stone,
Shelter of a wild-cherry tree.

O clams that are still fresh from mud!
O lobsters turning slowly red!
O delicate young Irish spud!
O corn whose husk has not been shed!

—CHRISTOPHER LAFARGE

Portrait—Sarah Josepha Hale

MARY'S LITTLE LAMB

NOW and then there flits across a few pages of history the distinct shadow of one whose influence forever changes those pages. Such a shadow is that which was cast by Sarah Josepha Buell Hale during the nineteenth century in America. Few women of today realize the extent to which they owe gratitude to Mrs. Hale, yet in some way every day we should be thankful for her long life devoted to our welfare.

Sarah Josepha Buell was born in Newport, New Hampshire, on April 30, 1788, of good sturdy pioneer New England parents. Because there were few schools for the education of girls at that time, little Sarah was tutored vigorously by her mother from the Bible, and from the works of Shakespeare, Milton, Addison, Robert Burns, and other writers whose works were seldom available to such book-hungry folk in faraway places. A brother who went to college at nearby Dartmouth also imparted to his sister all that he could of his school learning. At a time when women were considered quite unfit for teaching, Sarah acquired a position and succeeded remarkably as a Newport schoolteacher for seven years.

When she was twenty-five years old—an old maid for those times—Sarah married David Hale, a young Newport lawyer of a fine family. Although frail at the time of her marriage, she became strong with the encouragement of her husband in proper exercise and diet. In the evening, it was their pleasant habit to read and study together at their fireside. It was a happy marriage; the two were good companions.

Four children were born and another was on the way when the young father was stricken with pneumonia and died quite suddenly, leaving his wife with a family and no means to provide for them. Her greatest concern was a lack of funds with which to educate them.

Proud and resourceful, Sarah Hale wasted no time feeling sorry for herself. She soon launched into a career of writing, at that time an almost impossible career for a woman. She nevertheless pursued this career with vigor and success, as we shall see.

Her first publication was a book of verse, and although not notable, it was supported by friends and gave her the courage to try again. Her second published volume was called *Northwood, or Life North and South*, a moralizing tale of the problems of slavery. The book was of importance, coming at a time when sectional feelings were considerably aroused. It was an immediate success, and her future—and more important to her, the future education and welfare of her five children—was assured.

Not long after this, a Boston publisher whose name also happened to be Hale, Rev. John L. Hale, conducted a poetry contest, which our Sarah won. Rev. Hale invited her to become the editor of a new kind of magazine to be devoted solely to women, *The Ladies' Magazine*, and Sarah accepted the position, moving her family to Boston.

Sarah Hale then launched upon a crusade, as she expressed it, "to promote the reputation of my sex." It is difficult for us to believe now, with the plethora of magazines which are devoted to women and the home, that such an idea was quite revolutionary in 1828, and it was with considerable courage and high resolve that she undertook this work.

Since girls and women were virtually uneducated in those times, it being thought unnecessary, she began devoting her talent with the pen to the promotion of proper schooling for girls, including the employment of women as teachers. She hammered at this issue so vehemently that it was not long until she could see the ideas taking effect. She became a great force in the establishment of excellent schools and colleges for women, including Mount Holyoke and Smith colleges. Her crusade included property rights for women; better working conditions for women; abolition of child labor; establishment of nurseries and playgrounds for children; better conditions of health and sanitation; and better home management.

Sarah Hale didn't preach about these reforms. She had a subtle way of writing simply about her causes, assuming always that her readers had the intelligence to agree with her. Since her readers were principally women, it is quite certain that they did agree with her, and so the trick worked very well. We smile now to read that she advocated exercise for women such as swimming and horseback riding; bathing at least once a week; cleanliness in person and in dress. She was against featherbeds, airtight sleeping rooms, tight corsets, and exaggerated fashions.

Mrs. Hale edited *The Ladies' Magazine* for thirteen years. During this time her pen was never idle. She wrote a number of books on American life, manners, and characteristics. A charming little volume of Victorian verse called *Flora's Interpreter* on the symbolism of flowers was one of her published works. The book may still occasionally be found on the dusty shelves of secondhand bookstores or in a box of old books at a country auction. It includes several hand-colored engravings of flowers.

Sarah Hale believed vigorously that women should become more involved in righting the wrongs of the world, and she was soon to show that their powers in this regard were very great. In Boston the building of the Bunker Hill Monument had come to a halt for lack of funds, and it stood unfinished atop the hill, sad and neglected. Mrs. Hale's pen came to do battle for the cause, and she proposed organizing her women readers to raise the necessary money. She was not encouraged at all in this proposal, men in charge of the project being utterly scornful that anything they had failed in accomplishing could be better done by women. But in her clever way, Mrs. Hale persuaded them that women were intended to offer their help to men whenever they could.

In a second "Battle of Bunker Hill," then, she took firm aim, and so aroused her readers that in time they conducted "the great Fair" for the benefit of the unfinished monument. Here were exhibited and sold hand-made wares, the patterns and recipes for which had perhaps been found among the pages of *The Ladies' Magazine*. The Fair produced the necessary thirty thousand dollars and the Monument was completed. It was a great day for the ladies when the Bunker Hill Monument was finally dedicated!

Now and then Editor Hale devoted words in her magazine to a plea for the establishment of a National Day of Thanksgiving. For a time there seemed to be other more pressing things, however.

In Philadelphia an enterprising young man named Godey had ventured into the publishing business with a periodical called *Godey's Lady's Book* which was an immediate success. With an acumen which would do credit to the industrial giants of today and might now bring a frown from the Justice Department in Washington, he perceived that to get the editor he wanted, and to do away with the rival magazine which she was editing, he would have to buy out *The Ladies' Magazine*. This he did. So Sarah Josepha Hale, now a lady journalist of national fame, moved to Philadelphia and became the editor of *Godey's Lady's Book*.

Although this famous magazine has been remembered for the hand-colored fashion plates which were a part of each issue, Sarah Hale's contributions to the magazine were not fashion but editorship. Her own ideas of fashion were much simpler. No matter what the current vogue might be for bustles and bows, for hoops and ruffles, she advocated good taste always, and left the editing of the fashion department to Mr. Godey, her publisher. She dressed smartly in rich fabrics, but never exceeded her own dictates of taste.

She wrote on many subjects concerning the world of the American woman, and encouraged contributions to the pages of the *Lady's Book* from many of the best writers of the day. In spite of her goals for the general emancipation of women, she never lost sight of the woman's real place— in the home, as a mother, as an influence for good in her own family above everything else. The pages of the magazine were filled with copious advice on keeping a home and raising a family, as well as interesting her readers in championing many righteous causes. She loved picnics and promoted them vigorously as of benefit to the life of a family.

Once again she began her bombardment on the subject of a National Day of Thanksgiving. Finally President Lincoln, in November 1864, succumbed to the pleas of Editor Hale and her readers, and declared the last Thursday of November to be such a national Thanksgiving Day. Several attempts have been made to change the date, but none has succeeded, so firmly entrenched now is the American tradition of that day.

The busy editor of *Godey's Lady's Book* somehow found time to continue publishing other books, among them several books of cookery and of manners, an anthology of poetry, and an encyclopedia of *Distinguished Women* of all time. At the age of eighty-nine she finally put down her pen and retired, well deserving a rest from her many years of work.

Among the works of Sarah Josepha Hale was a book published about 1830 which was called *Poems for Our Children*, written to "please and instruct, to induce you to love truth and goodness." Among these poems was one called "Mary's Lamb." Like the little lamb, this poem has followed me all my days. I can do no less than give tribute to the charming, talented, industrious lady who wrote it.

Mary's Lamb

Mary had a little lamb,
  Its fleece was white as snow,
And everywhere that Mary went
  The lamb was sure to go;

He followed her to school one day—
  That was against the rule,
It made the children laugh and play,
  To see a lamb in school.

And so the Teacher turned him out,
  But still he lingered near,
And waited patiently about,
  Till Mary did appear;

And then he ran to her, and laid
  His head upon her arm,
As if he said— "I'm not afraid—
  You'll keep me from all harm."

"What makes the lamb love Mary so?"
  The eager children cry—
"Oh, Mary loves the lamb, you know,"
  The Teacher did reply;—

"And you each gentle animal
  In confidence may bind,
And make them follow at your call,
  If you are always *kind*."

AUGUST

Birthstone and Birthdays

August's Birthstone is the *Sardonyx* or the *Cornelia,* meaning *Felicity.*

1	16
2	17
3	18
4	19
5	20
6	21
7	22
8	23
9	24
10	25
11	26
12	27
13	28
14	29
15	30
	31

Flower

THE POPPY
Papaver

THE only native New England member of the Poppy family is the Blood-root, the delicate flower which blooms in spring in abundance in open, rich woods. Its pure white petals are not really petals at all, but are called sepals by botanists. Most poppies have milky juice in their stems, but the name of our native variety, the Bloodroot, came from the deep red color of its stem and root juice. It has been suggested that the name "Poppy" comes from the fact that the flowers open quickly with a "pop," and the petals drop off just as quickly, with another "pop." But to be truthful, it probably came from the Latin name of the family, *Papaver*.

Bloodroot plants are easily transplanted into corners of the wild garden and multiply very satisfactorily into large clumps. They are self-seeding.

Other poppies from foreign lands have been known in New England gardens since at least 1760 when Oriental poppies were advertised for sale in a Boston paper. The fact that this member of the family should be divided or propagated by root-cutting in August for best results is the only reason I can think of for its being named the August flower by sentimentalists. Some of the annual varieties bloom in gardens all summer long, including early August, and furnish a bright spot of color. These are easy to raise, but have a long taproot which makes the plant difficult to move with success, and so seeds should be planted in early spring where they are to bloom.

As everyone knows, opium is made from poppies, which probably is the reason for its Victorian meaning of Consolation or Forgetfulness. According to the herbalist Nicholas Culpeper, an infusion of poppies cured everything from warts to jaundice, from the plague to headaches; could be put "into hollow teeth to ease the pain and has been found by experience to ease the pains of the gout." It also cured ague and "phrenzies," according to Mr. Culpeper.

> But pleasures are like poppies spread,
> You seize the flower, its bloom is shed;
> Or like the snow falls in the river
> A moment white, then melts forever.
>
> —ROBERT BURNS, "Tam o' Shanter"

Bird

THE HERMIT THRUSH
Hylocichla guttata

With what a clear
And ravishing sweetness sang the plaintive thrush!
I love to hear his delicate rich voice,
Chanting through all the gloomy day, when loud
Amid the trees is dropping the big rain,
And gray mists wrap the hills; for age the sweeter
His song is when the day is sad and dark.

—HENRY WADSWORTH LONGFELLOW

SOME of the country folk call the Hermit Thrush by the name of "fife-bird," which harks back through many generations to the time when the clear mellow notes of the simple fife was a musical sound most familiar and dear to the earliest settlers (and it was the instrument which so stirringly piped the way of the countrymen to fight for their freedom at Concord and Lexington and Bunker Hill). There are other affectionate names for this prima donna of the woodlands which attempt to link it with the sound of its voice: Bellbird, Angelbird, Song Thrush.

How can one describe a birdsong so mellow, so liquid, so divine in quality? The great naturalist Burroughs said the thrush's song is the finest sound in nature, an instrument of silver, a voice of calm sweet solemnity, of deep solemn joy. Ask someone who has heard the song to describe it and he will use words which are themselves beautiful but are still inadequate—words such as flutelike, pure silver, liquid gold, serene, ethereal, floating melody, a sweet rippling. Truly the Hermit Thrush sings the finest birdsong of all.

The song always begins with a little introduction, a calm, meditative note which almost seems to give the pitch for the rich cadences which follow. The music comes in unhurried triplets and fifths, sublimely filling the air with threads of tone. There is a heavenly divine quality to the voice as it drifts in a dreamy way out of the woods into the garden where we sit at evening in hushed wonder at the improvised melodies, the outpouring of lovely song.

In summer, one does not often see a Hermit Thrush, though we wait for his matchless angelus in summer twilights. He is a bird more often heard than seen, for he prefers the solitude of the deep woods to the haunts of man. His habitat may be low, wooded, swampy lands or dense, cool, upper woodlands and brushy lanes. He builds his neat cup of a nest in the crotches or branches of low trees, sometimes on a little weedy hummock of ground, and makes it of moss, plant fibers, leaves, and fine rootlets, sometimes pine needles. There will usually be four or five blue-green eggs and there may be two or more broods a season, so that the mating songs are heard over a rather long period of time.

He feeds on the floor of the woods, turning over bits of moss and old leaves in his search for a meal. In autumn he will occasionally come into the dooryard looking for a feast of worms, insects, or grubs. He sometimes winters over in southern New England, when he resorts to a vegetarian diet of berries found in parks, margins of woods, and shrubby roadsides where berries are plentiful. He may partake of small bits of meat placed on the ground near shrubby places in the gardens of country houses when snow and storm cover his natural sources of food.

His protective coloration is perfect, as he is brown on the head and shoulders, with a reddish-brown tail, and he is marked with dark-brown heart-shaped spots on his white throat and breast. The Hermit Thrushes are loathe to leave the nest when they are sitting on eggs or protecting young birds, and their coloring blends into their background so well that they are not seen even though one may pass very close to the nest on which they are watchfully sitting.

The Hermit Thrush is a dignified, graceful, elegant bird, and even its habits of eating are dainty and well mannered. Its disposition is gentle and peaceful with no fighting characteristics whatever, as if it trusted all creatures implicitly. It is also said to be highly intelligent. Its warning call sounds sharp and anxious but in no way belligerent, and when alarmed it slowly raises its tail to an almost perpendicular position, one of its distinguishing habits.

Again turning to Mr. Burroughs to describe this lovely bird, he said, "In grace and elegance of manner he has no equal. Such a gentle, high-bred air, such inimitable ease and composure in his flight and movement. He is a poet in every word and deed. He has regal grace . . . plain, yet rich in color."

His near cousins, the wood thrush, the brown thrasher, the robin and bluebird, and the shy veery all have lovely voices and most of them have fine manners, but none equals the Hermit Thrush.

At the end of a busy and exciting mountain cookout, we once lingered long past sunset to enjoy the clear mountain air and the superb view. From the woods around us came first the gentle, quiet, sweet song of the veery which spirals down the scale, a sound like "Whée-ew, whée-ew, whée-ew, whée-ew." Like the Thrush's, the veery's song varies in volume so that it is very difficult to tell how far away the bird may be.

Then from another direction came floating into the mountain stillness the liquid bell song of the Hermit Thrush, pure as spring water, a hymn of eventide. The sweet voice sang on and on, lingering after all else was still, the twilight faded, and the stars had begun to shine. At last it, too, was still. A memorable concert indeed.

In the swamp, in secluded recesses,
A shy and hidden bird is warbling a song.
Solitary, the thrush,
The hermit, withdrawn to himself, voiding
    the settlements,
Sings by himself a song.

—WALT WHITMAN,
    "When Lilacs Last in
    the Door-yard Bloom'd"

Good Bees Make Good Blueberries

The jeweled sea and the deeps of the air,
All heaven and earth are good and fair,
Ferns at my feet and the mullein's spike,
And the soaring gull I love alike;
With the schooner's grace as she leans to the tide
The soul within me is satisfied.

—CELIA THAXTER

SUMMER falters. Mornings taste of autumn; evenings close in earlier, quietly, no longer filled with melodies of garden birds. Only the thrush may still be heard singing, or a robin calling. A cricket chirps at the door-rock and cicadas forecast frost ("six weeks from the first song of the cicada"). Swallows gather on telephone wires and sweep through the late summer air to gather such feasts as they may. Elderberries and blueberries are dead ripe. Goldenrod lifts its fringed blossoms over the stone walls. Butterflies hover over the hollows and ditches where joe-pye weed blooms in soft purple drifts. In years gone by, to cure fevers tea was made from joe-pye weed and its sister plant, the white boneset.

In the woods' damp shady places, Indian pipe rises in its ghostly white and we stoop to examine it in wonder and delight. British soldier or "red-coat" moss brightens gray decaying tree stumps; bird's-nest fungus spreads its dainty cups in a bed of leaf mold. At the brook, a doe lifts her proud lovely head, listening, then stoops to drink of the cool water. With a flick of her white tail, she bounds off through the trees and as we watch her grace and beauty we say a silent prayer for her. She, like her fawns, is our special joy and we live in dread for her of the gunshots of the hunting season.

At sunrise, predicting a fair day, spider webs are strung with drops of early morning dew. "It'll be a good day for paintin'," our old neighbor Jim Keegan used to say as he set up his ladders and made ready to paint a house or barn on such a morning.

Spiders are some of nature's most astonishing architects. They erect a strong staging for fashioning their webs, which they snip away with a built-in scissor arrangement after the inner web is completed. The framework of the web and the radiating lines are strong, secure, and taut; the spiral lines are sticky and wet and shiny and elastic, stretching to hold firmly a struggling prey caught in the silky threads. As they weave, spiders manipulate with their hind legs the threads which they exude from within their own bodies. With a finger, I trace the radial lines of a spider web and admire its precision, beauty, and strength. When it is laden with dew, I pause a moment to marvel at its shimmering delicacy.

Yes, blueberries are ripe. A day in August is the day to go blueberrying. A full lunch basket, a blue sky and soft breeze, and a favorite blueberry pail are the only requisites. Much of New England is prime blueberry country. Wild and sweet, low-bush and high-bush, they grow along roadsides, in pastures, thickets, and rocky fields. The low-bush berries ripen a little earlier than the others. Picking them can be backbreaking unless one sits down in the middle of a patch and reaches all around. Some say these are the sweetest. High-bush berries sometimes grow to be man-sized shrubs and picking on such a bush is easy. The season is a long one in a lush patch, usually stretching over the months of July and August, even September in the north.

Blueberries are actually nearly black, but they are covered with a silvery bloom which gives them an illusive blue color. The seasoned blueberry picker notes that berries on the sheltered north side of a bush may be darker, with less bloom than those on the south side, so he will reason that the bloom is put there by the touch of sun and rain, dew, and gentle wind.

The picker hooks the pail to his belt and vigorously goes about his business with both hands. One who is deft can hold the branch with one hand, pick a great handful with the other, then sort out the leaves, withered berries, and stems before he drops the perfect ones into the bucket. He will have more berries at the end of the day than his companion who grabs in haste and whose pailful is laced with leaves and sticks.

A farmer's wife once told me, "Blueberryin' is just like milkin' a cow; you pull the berries off the branch just the same way." A bunch of twenty-five or thirty blueberries is a good handful to grasp and pull with a quick gentle motion that does not tear the berries.

In New Jersey, Miss Elizabeth White years ago decided to harness the wild blueberry, and the hybrid cultivated blueberries were the result of her experiments. To get this wonder berry, wild bushes were mated until Miss White's specifications were met. The very first matings were of native New England bushes which produced unusually large, sweet berries.

Blueberries make an ornamental as well as a fruitful plant for home growing, if the soil is naturally acid. They are a very hardy plant with small, dark, glossy leaves. In the spring the bushes are covered with little clusters of delicate cream and pink flowers; and in the autumn the leaves turn scarlet, making brilliant flashes of color. Wild bushes do not grow satisfactorily in cultivation. For the home garden, it is best to buy nursery stock which has been hybridized, and two or more varieties are needed to insure cross-pollination. They prefer a loose soil in which there has been mixed plenty of peat moss, and they enjoy an annual mulch of decayed oak leaves, pine needles, or sawdust to keep the roots moist during dry months.

Blueberries produce a jam which can hardly be surpassed for deliciousness on baking powder biscuits, corn bread, or as a topping for ice cream. They are the easiest of fruits to can and freeze. For canning, one has only to pack the fresh, whole berries carefully but firmly into hot glass jars, filling to the top of the jar. No sugar, no water. They can be sealed immediately with self-seal tops which have been immersed in boiling water; then the filled jars are processed in boiling water to cover for fifteen minutes. Remove from the kettle, hold firmly, and tighten the jar top to make sure of seal. Cool and store. They keep perfectly for several years, and when the jar is opened, some of the berries (if not processed overlong) will still have on them the bloom of the day they were picked.

For freezing, blueberries can be spread evenly on cooky sheets, frozen, then scooped into containers and stored in the freezer. On a winter's day, how satisfying to remove from the containers just enough berries for a pie or hot muffins or pancakes.

Someone has said that one smells rather than tastes blueberries. Certainly when baked they are their own rich reward in fragrance, reminiscent of the summer days in which they ripen, of the pleasant sound of bees ("good bees make good blueberries" is an old adage), of the benison of sun and wind, of the call of a ruddy-sided towhee who keeps us company. (Does he say "Drink your tea" or does he say "Brush your teeth" as a four-year-old friend of ours named Karen thoughtfully suggested?)

Blueberries are made into jam and pie and muffins, as we have just said. They are also made into betty, slump, grunt, cobbler, shortcake, fool, and flummery. Our own favorite dish is Blueberry Topsy Turvy Cake with plenty of rich cream or homemade vanilla ice cream. Blueberry festivals are held where pies are made in quantities, long rows of them, warm and tantalizing; stacks of pancakes, baskets of muffins. No family reunion in New England would be complete without quantities of blueberry treats prepared by good country cooks who compete good-naturedly with each other in producing wonderful food for their gathering clans.

The Bradfords, the Beans, the Howlands, the Hardys, the Wings, the Aldens, and many other old families assemble in their native towns from near and far for family reunions. In New Hampshire during August's official Old Home Week, each town celebrates and welcomes its former residents. There are parades and bands and speeches and picnics and ballgames and suppers and horseshoe-pitching contests and hymn sings and barbershop singers and—blueberries.

At a family gathering not long ago, a friend of ninety summers, who remembers with keenness and good humor the family events in which he has participated over the years, told the story of visiting his grandmother when he was a small boy. Among those members of the Southmayd clan who were collected there to enjoy his grandmother's fine country cooking was a relative who sat down at the table with a healthy appetite. For dessert, he had a piece of blackberry pie; then another piece; then a third piece of the delectable pie. At last, the hostess noticed John looking thoughtful and she said, "John, will you have another piece of blackberry pie?" He said, "No, thank you, ma'am. I never cared much for blackberry pie. The seeds stick in my teeth." And he reached for a slice of blueberry pie.

No better word picture of family reunions has ever been painted than in Sarah Orne Jewett's *The Country of the Pointed Firs*, which tells of the Bowden family reunion on the Maine coast one August in the last century.

The Bowdens arrived by schooner, sailboat, and rowboat; by buggy, carriage, and wagon; and some on foot. Almira Todd, her old mother, and their guest put on their best bonnets, then hired a grocer's wagon and ancient white horse to transport them to their reunion. All along the dusty country road they stopped to visit old friends, to refresh themselves with fresh doughnuts, and to wave to those watching from their porches. Nowadays, those who return to New England for family reunions come by car, by plane, perhaps some by boat or train, even motorcycle. Few come on foot. The Bowdens wouldn't have believed it possible to come so far as we do now.

There is something almost instinctive in the congregating of a large family at reunion time. Like the gathering of swallows for their flight to the south; like the runs of the shad and the salmon to their ancestral spawning places; like the twilight return of the cattle to their barns, we come home now and then to renew our family heritage in rites which seem as old as the hills of New England. From the tip of Cape Cod to the Berkshires, from urban Connecticut to the smallest village of the northeastern corner of Maine, great families gather in pride and excitement to relive their past and exult in their future.

Except for the mode of dress and the addition of some sophisticated entertainment such as a lecture by a learned member of the family about a distinguished forebear, family reunions haven't changed much in the last hundred years. We still remember with appreciation and sadness those who no longer appear; still treat our elders with dignified reverence, respect, and love; still reminisce in humor and delight; still compare notes on family history and brag about the children. As in the Bowden family, we still spread a "noble feast, with an elegant ingenuity in the form of pies" and compete in setting out an array of home cookery to please every gathered cousin, uncle, and hungry child.

There is no lack of produce in August gardens, the best of which is saved for the fairs and the reunions. Jars of golden mustard pickles and crisp green cucumber slices wait in rows in the cool cellar. String beans and corn relish are counted by the dozens of jars. Jams and jellies in sparkling colors await such special occasions. Herbs are hanging from the rafters in the warm dry shed, soon to be pulverized for winter's use, but green herbs are plentiful in the garden for fresh salads: lettuce, parsley, tarragon and chives, savory and thyme and chervil. There is no lack of garden stuff for family reunions, no indeed. Even the tomatoes are ripe, the better to flavor a casserole of summer vegetables.

CASEROLE OF SUMMER SQUASH

2 Tbs. olive oil	1 Tbs. salt
About 2 lbs. of summer squash, washed and cut into cubes or small slices	2 Tbs. sugar
	1 tsp. dry mustard
1 white onion, peeled and chopped	1 Tbs. dried oregano (savory, marjoram, or thyme may be used instead)
3 large (or 5 or 6 medium) tomatoes, peeled and quartered	1 cup breadcrumbs or cracker crumbs
2 tsp. fresh-ground pepper	1 cup grated Vermont cheese
	4 Tbs. butter

Preheat oven to 350°. Parboil squash for 5 minutes, then drain. Put olive oil in 3-quart baking dish or casserole (or 2 smaller dishes). Put in the squash, onions, and tomatoes. Mix together the salt, pepper, sugar, mustard, herbs, breadcrumbs, and one-half of the grated cheese. Spread mixture over top of the vegetables. Dot with the butter. Cover the casserole and bake for 50 minutes. Remove cover, scatter the other half of the grated cheese over the top, and return uncovered to the oven until cheese is melted and browned.

Serves 12.

BLUEBERRY JAM

Pick over and crush enough blueberries to make 9 cups. Add 1 cup of water and boil in a large kettle until berries are very soft. Stir in 6 cups sugar and boil to the jelly stage (or until jelly thermometer reaches 220°). Add juice of 1 lemon and stir in thoroughly. Pour the jam into hot sterilized jam jars, wipe any spilled jam off rims of jars and seal at once with self-sealing lids. As is true of most fruit jellies and jams, blueberry jam is better if the fruit is just ripe, not overripe, and it jells more easily then.

BLUEBERRY TOPSY TURVY CAKE

¼ cup butter   1½ cups blueberries
¼ cup light brown sugar   Juice of 1 lemon
¼ cup white sugar

Melt butter in an 8-inch round or square cake pan (2 inches deep). Add sugars, stir well, and remove from heat. Cool for 5 minutes, then spread blueberries over mixture, and squeeze lemon juice over.

Stir together the following dry ingredients:

1⅓ cups sifted cake flour   ½ tsp. cinnamon
2 tsp. baking powder   ½ tsp. nutmeg
Pinch of salt   ¾ cup white sugar

Cream ¼ cup soft butter; add dry ingredients, then add:

1 egg
½ cup milk (or half milk and
    half sour cream for richer
    batter)
2 tsp. vanilla

Stir until well blended but do not overbeat. Pour the batter over blueberries in the pan. Bake in preheated 350° oven for 40–50 minutes or until cake springs back when touched lightly with finger. Cool cake in pan 5 minutes, then put a serving plate over the pan and turn all upside down. Let stand a moment until cake falls out of pan, then remove pan. Serve warm with sweetened whipped cream.

WHITLATCH CORN RELISH

In a large kettle of boiling salted water, put freshly picked sweet corn, bring again to a boil, and cook for 10 minutes. Cool the corn and cut the

SARAH ORNE JEWETT

kernels off the cob, enough to make 2 quarts (8 cups) of cut-off kernels. Throw away the cooking water.

In the kettle combine the following ingredients and boil hard for 5 minutes:

1 quart finely chopped cabbage	1 quart vinegar
1 cup each finely chopped sweet red pepper, green pepper, and onion	1 Tbs. each salt, celery seed, mustard seed
1½ cups water	1½ tsp. turmeric
	2 Tbs. dry mustard

Add the cooked corn to the kettle, cook for another 10 minutes, stirring well to mix. Pack in sterilized hot jars, leaving a half-inch at top of jar.

It takes 12–14 medium ears to make 1 quart cut-off corn, or about 2 dozen ears for this recipe. Makes 8 or 9 pints.

ETTA SCOTT'S "PRETTY PICKLES"

Peel and remove seeds from large green or ripe cucumbers. Dice, and measure out 2 quarts of the diced cucumbers. Chop 2 peeled onions and 2 sweet red peppers, and add to the cucumbers. Mix in 2 Tbs. salt. Cover the mixture with cold water and let stand 3 hours. Drain and discard the water.

Make a syrup of 2 cups sugar, 2 cups vinegar, 1 tsp. tumeric, and heat to boiling. Add the cucumber mixture and cook until transparent. Ladle into hot sterilized jars and seal.

This is every cook's opinion
No savory dish without an onion.
But lest your kissing should be spoiled
Your onions must be fully boiled.
—JONATHAN SWIFT

Portrait—Sarah Orne Jewett

THE COUNTRY OF THE POINTED FIRS

"BEING a New Englander, it is natural that I should first speak about the weather." So wrote Sarah Orne Jewett at the beginning of one of her stories. She had a way of talking about the weather, about the gentle village folk, about the sights and sounds of the sea, about the Maine shore and countryside that is like a breath of fresh salt air through an open window. To read her stories today is to go back a hundred or more years along the Maine coast to a time when fishermen and sailors were busy with their tasks at net and rope and tiller; when housewives collected simples from the fields and woods around their cottages; when life was unhurried and the weather was of first importance but was accepted as it came.

Sarah Orne Jewett was born in South Berwick, Maine, on September 3, 1849. The glories of the pretty riverport town of Berwick were fading, the harbor becoming deserted, and the farms dwindling into neglect.

Sarah was a rather precocious little girl, being less interested in school than in the stories her grandfather and father told her of more romantic and colorful days in her quiet neighborhood. She loved riding with her doctor father in his carriage as he called on patients in the villages and countryside around their home. She loved watching the daily life of the village, especially at the store where she could see planks of wood, maple syrup, and eggs being brought to exchange for flour and salt and cotton and tea. She pored over the fine leather-bound volumes in her father's library and knew every book on its shelves. She watched, listened, remembered all that she learned, and was able to record it in her stories as she grew up.

Often as her father called on patients she would sit in their kitchens waiting for him, listening to their conversations about the simple things that filled their lives. Sometimes she climbed a hill or walked down a pasture lane to absorb the songs of birds and the look of the trees against the sky, the wonder of flowers and ferns unfolding in the dry leaves of the Maine woodlands. She remembered all these.

As Sarah Orne Jewett grew up, conditions were changing in Maine even more. The clean pure air blowing in across the fertile fields was now sometimes cloudy with the smoke of industry. Rows of drab gray mill houses were replacing the fine colonial mansions and the pretty cottages along the streets. Woods were being cut down, and where tall straight trees had grown for many years were left only acres of slash and dead branches. The shipyard which had brought such romance and prosperity to Berwick was sagging. Those who still clung to their weather-beaten cottages and dilapidated farms were living not in the present nor looking ahead to the future, but were remembering the past.

Sarah was a frail youngster, but because she enjoyed being out-of-doors she lived a happy, wholesome life. One day she began writing verses and stories which seemed to tell themselves in her mind. At last she had the courage to send a story to the editor of a children's magazine. She could not bear to sign her own name so she signed the name Alice Eliot. Everyone at home was pledged to secrecy, but of course when she asked at the post office if there was any mail for Alice Eliot, the postmistress knew there was something mysterious going on. The editor of the magazine accepted the story at once, and the next step was made easier. She wrote another story and this time sent it in to the editor of *The Atlantic Monthly*, who accepted it with few changes; and so Alice Eliot became Sarah Orne Jewett once more and her success began to widen.

With success she found that her life became more complicated. She ventured away quite often, going to Boston, New York, and Philadelphia to visit friends. But she always felt that home was the place where her thoughts collected themselves for stories, and she returned there to write.

She became quite a regular contributor to *The Atlantic Monthly*. She had met the editors who encouraged her to write more. Thanks to her remarkably keen insight and memory and to the companionship she had shared with her father, she was well steeped in her environment. The people and background about which she wrote were so deeply etched in her mind that they flowed onto paper with ease. The salty talk of the fisherfolk, the homely wisdom of the housewives, the feel and look of nature all came to her stories as clearly as the fragrance of bayberry to one who walks the shore on a warm sunny day.

By the time she was twenty-eight, a book of Sarah's sketches had been successfully published. She had met James Russell Lowell and Thomas Bailey Aldrich and Oliver Wendell Holmes and Celia Thaxter, and was in correspondence with people of letters everywhere. Her social contacts were increasing. Still she seemed to cling to the past and the familiar things of home.

Soon after the success of her first book, she was to lose the father so dear to her and to realize all that he had meant to her. It was a loss of the deepest sadness to her. Seeming to need companionship to help ease her loss, she formed a close friendship with the young intelligent widow of a Boston publisher which was to be of lasting influence in her life.

There is no evidence that Sarah Orne Jewett ever gave any serious consideration to marriage. She loved writing, and found such deep satisfaction in it as to need no other outlet. Attractive, warmhearted, she was a pretty woman with brown lively eyes and a natural charm by which she made friendships easily. She liked to dress fashionably and attend parties. At length she and her friend Mrs. Fields went abroad. This was a rich experience for her and was to be repeated a number of times. But she always returned to Berwick to write the stories which filled her mind, amid the people and the countryside she knew and loved so well.

It is easy to picture her return after a long absence to the lovely old
house which had been her grandfather's. She would waken in the morning
with the fresh breeze from seaward blowing through the open window; she
would hear the early morning songs of the birds and the familiar sounds of
the town. She would get up to take a long walk across a pasture or through
the woods or along the river to refresh her mind; she would cut flowers from
her own garden and arrange them in a bowl on her desk, and pour a cup
of tea for a friend who might drop in to welcome her back. This was home.
In a day or two, she would sit at her desk and begin to write.

The years passed. The world she had known as a child was gone. Only
her own house was the same. The friends who had inspired and encouraged
her were going, and no one of the same warmth was taking their place.
She was writing with increasing beauty of the old rural life in New England
and it filled her mind always. At times she was not well enough to travel
or to write, which left her impatient to do all that she could while her
strength lasted. She had matured, as had her way of writing. She described
the things she had known without an overrichness of words so that the
pictures had clarity and light, qualities which today seem so refreshing in
her stories.

At forty-seven there began to take form in her mind the story of *The
Country of the Pointed Firs,* which many believe is one of the great classics
of the literature of New England. There is no particular plot to this story;
it is a simple tale of life on the Maine coast in the nineteenth century which
involves the fishing villages, the "Dunnet Landings" of the area, and their
people. Told by a visiting schoolteacher who stays for the summer with
Almira Todd, the herb-gatherer, the story unfolds to include Mis' Todd's
brother William and her mother Mis' Blackett, the sprightly old lady who
lived on nearby Green Island. The teacher learns to know some of the secrets
of the herbs which Mis' Todd gathers, sometimes by the light of the moon;
and talks with old Captain Tilley about his "dear girl," now long gone; and

attends the Bowden family reunion, a great event in the lives of the Dunnet Landing people. There is captured in this story the essence of the Maine coast which no one else has pictured with such simple eloquence.

In 1901 Bowdoin College conferred upon her the first Litt.D. degree it had ever given to a woman. It was from this college that her father had graduated in 1834, and of which he had for a time been a staff member. Her sister Mary attended the Commencement exercises and the two sisters were very touched when the chaplain mentioned their father in his prayer for the occasion. It was a happy time for Sarah and she was proud of the honor.

One afternoon she took some friends to drive with her in her carriage. The carriage lurched sharply and Sarah was thrown out, landing with considerable force, injuring her head and spine. It was many months before she had the strength to lift her pen, and then only to write letters. The injury left her with an inability to collect her thoughts completely and she was never again to write for publication. More than ever, she took all the joy and happiness she could from her home in Berwick, from such of her old friends and neighbors as were left, from the woods and fields and gardens nearby to which she could still go for a breath of quiet and peace. Friends came from far and near to see her and visit with her. But one day she was to write to her friend Mrs. Fields, "Dear, I do not know what to do with me," and it was apparent that her spirit and vitality were ebbing. On June 24, 1909, in the room she loved so much, she died, "leaving the lilac bushes still green and growing, and all the chairs in their places." They are in their places still, as her home is open to those who would like to visit it.

Her gentle stories of old Maine, of the sailing ships and the fishing ports and the quaint country people are filled with serenity and warmth which is "like an autumn sunset." It is New England at its enduring poetic best.

The month was August, and I had seen the color of the islands change from the fresh green of June to a sun-burnt brown that made them look like stone, except where the dark green of the spruces and fir balsam kept the tint that even winter storms might deepen but not fade. The few wind-bent trees on Shell-heap Island were mostly dead and gray, but there were some low-growing bushes, and a stripe of light green ran along just above the shore, which I knew to be wild morning-glories.

—SARAH ORNE JEWETT,
The Country of
the Pointed Firs

SEPTEMBER

Birthstone and Birthdays

September's Birthstone is the *Sapphire*, for *Good Fortune*.

1	16
2	17
3	18
4	19
5	20
6	21
7	22
8	23
9	24
10	25
11	26
12	27
13	28
14	29
15	30

Flower

THE GOLDENROD
Solidago

VICTORIAN ladies did not dignify the common Goldenrod of the fields by listing it among their favorite flowers. Nor in fact did they consider it for planting in gardens. It just grew. Everywhere. In fields and pastures, along roadsides, and at the edge of the woods. Holly was the flower which in Great-Grandmother's day was designated as the September plant, but since we in our day associate holly so definitely with Christmas decorating, I have taken the liberty of substituting one of my own favorite field flowers, the Goldenrod, in place of Great-Grandmother's choice for September.

Goldenrod is much more valued in Europe than it is at home. It is one of our natives which was taken across the Atlantic to be planted in the finest of European flower gardens. I have seen it used there as a background plant and for a glow of sunny color in garden borders.

There are many kinds of Goldenrod, most of which grow wild in New England. In August and September, they arise in feathery golden plumes in company with purple New England asters. The two flowers have a particular fitness for autumn, harmonizing with the brilliant colors of that season.

Goldenrod has a habit of coming up year after year wherever it can establish itself, despite the farmers' scythes and the cattle's grazing. It is useful to those who like to dye their own yarns for spinning and weaving, and to flower-arrangers for dried bouquets. Picked when flower buds are just opening, it can be used very effectively with other fall flowers in fresh arrangements.

The goldenrod is one of the fairy, magical
flowers; it grows not up to seek human love . . .
but to mark to the discerning what wealth lies
hid in the secret caves of earth.

—MARGARET FULLER

Bird

THE RUBY-THROATED HUMMINGBIRD
Archilochus colubris

A flash of harmless lightning,
A mist of rainbow dyes,
The burnished sunbeams brightning,
From flower to flower he flies.
— JOHN B. TABB

HUMMINGBIRDS and flowers go together like summertime and fireflies; like rainbows and sunshine. The easiest way of attracting these exquisite tiny birds is to grow flowers, as they come to every old-fashioned garden of New England each year as surely as the summer. Honeysuckle and clematis vines climbing over cottage porches; trumpet-flowers scrambling over old stone walls; narcissus, columbine, bluebell, sage and mint, larkspur, roses and phlox in neat borders in dooryards; lilac bushes growing in profusion against ancient weathered barns—these are the places where the hummingbirds dine, like the bees:

Seeing only what is fair,
Sipping only what is sweet.
— RALPH WALDO EMERSON

This incredibly tiny bird—the smallest of all birds—comes of a large family, but only the Ruby-throated Hummingbird is known on the East

Coast and in New England. It leaves us in September to spend the winter with many of its cousins in Mexico and Central America, and in doing so flies two thousand miles or more. About five hundred miles of this journey is across the open water of the Gulf of Mexico without a stop. How can this be true of such a minute creature which weighs about as much as a dime and is less than four inches long from tip of bill to tip of tail? The answer is that he has tremendous flower power! It is believed that in spite of its tiny size, the Hummingbird can stoke up, storing food and energy for its long gulf flight by eating well beforehand of the best-known energy-producing food—honey from flowers—and protein from the millions of tiny bugs it devours, such as aphids and plant lice. Since their wings move so unbelievably fast in flight—from fifty up to two hundred times a second on occasion —this feat of storing strength and energy for the migration is another in the long list of wonders about this wee sprite of a bird.

It is said that a Hummingbird will visit from one thousand to two thousand flowers a day, and in addition eats many small insects which it catches in the air. The bird is especially attracted to red or orange flowers and will inevitably visit a red geranium, monarda, or a fuchsia blossom before it delves into a blue or yellow flower. It dips into the calyx of the flowers to sip the nectar and if a flower such as a tulip seems too deep for its long bill, it will go to the base of the petals, push them aside, and drink from between the petals. Although the bill of the Hummingbird seems to be long for its size, its tongue is even longer, the better for tasting from such deep-cupped flowers as columbine, bluebells, and trumpet-flowers.

Feathers of the Hummingbirds are iridescent and change color with the reflection of light. There are green feathers on the back, sides, wings, and head, the iridescence being particularly brilliant on the sides of the head. The ruby-red throat of the male is the special distinguishing mark of this jeweled bird, and it gleams with dazzling brilliance, especially when he is courting his lady-love.

His courtship performance is breathtaking. As the lady of his choice sits preening on a little branch of tree or bush, the male begins his courtship flight through the air in long swings back and forth, as if he were a glittering pendant swinging from the sky by a long silken spider thread. He loops and dives and shoots through the air in wonderful maneuvers which surpass those of all other flying creatures. He has the capacity to turn his wings to change direction in a flash, to hover in the air (like a helicopter, the bird books say), to brake instantly when he chooses. He sings no pretty song, but utters a good many high-pitched little cries, as he courts or feeds or when alarmed. The fast movement of his wings creates the humming sound which is the reason for his name. He is heard before he is seen as a rule.

After the mating, the male goes off somewhere to sip nectar at his favorite taverns (perhaps even to find another lady, for he is not known for his fidelity), leaving the job of building the nest, incubating the eggs, and rearing the young to the female. She builds a beautiful tiny nest about the size of an apricot half, saddling it on the limb of a tree and fastening it securely with spider silk. The nest is composed of leaves and flower petals, fluffy down and feathers, fine hair and delicate fronds of fern. It is so well camouflaged with moss and lichens that it is exceedingly difficult to find. The two white eggs are like pearls, and there are usually two broods a year. The newborn birds are tiny, like little bees. The mother feeds them by digesting the food, regurgitating it, and pumping it deep into the throats of her youngsters.

Hummingbirds have other unusual characteristics which make them fascinating. They get along well with people, so long as they are not disturbed. We breakfast under the apple tree on fair mornings, and the Hummingbirds always join us, crash-diving into the apple blossoms, petunias, columbines, and herb flowers which surround us. They don't get along very well with other birds, even their own kind. Brave but jealous, they will duel even to the death if a rival interferes with courtship or feeding privileges or threatens any danger. They will fearlessly attack larger birds and even animals on provocation.

It is well worthwhile for entertainment to provide vials filled with sugar water in the garden to attract Hummingbirds. If they seem to quarrel over the rights to use such feeders, the vials may be spaced more widely and more feeders provided. A word of warning—the mixture in the vials should not be overly sweet, as too much refined sugar can injure their tiny digestive systems. One part sugar to two parts water boiled together five minutes plus a few drops of red food coloring is about the right proportion. The mixture should be freshened every few days, especially in warm weather. Hummingbirds may visit such feeders every fifteen minutes or so.

I have never seen a Hummingbird come to our birdbath, but they will often fly through the arc of a sprinkler, and they love to bathe in leaves wet with dew.

Country people say a Hummingbird brings good luck. So it does, for it is good luck indeed just to have one near, to watch its amazing flight patterns, its sipping at the flowers, its dazzling color in the sunlight.

What heavenly tints in mingling radiance fly!
Each rapid movement gives a different dye;
Like scales of burnished gold they dazzling show,
Now sink to shade, now like a furnace glow!

—ALEXANDER WILSON

Old Roads Winding

The Summer comes and the Summer goes;
  Wild-flowers are fringing the dusty lanes,
  The swallows go darting through fragrant rains,
Then, all of a sudden—it snows.
                              —THOMAS BAILEY ALDRICH

THERE is the warmth of summer in a September day; and the cool of autumn in the evenings. Rains are soft and smell of dried flowers and mushrooms. But a quick flurry of snow can blow across the North Field in the wake of a cold wave. A rainbow may span the pasture or the northern lights lighten the darkness of night with shimmering waves of color. The harvest moon may shine in orange serenity on shocks of corn and stacks of hay, or black clouds may scud anxiously across an angry sky. Blue waves of the Atlantic may wash quietly along the deserted sandy beaches, or rise in hurricane fury, pounding rocky coasts, devastating, destroying.

September is a month to be carefree. I can take off my apron, exchange my sneakers for a pair of shoes with heels, throw a coat of tweed over my arm and investigate the rest of the world with a clear conscience. Sometimes it's a far-off world I explore. From a balcony overlooking the blue Mediterranean, we have watched the sailboats drift in the breeze while we ate raspberry soufflé tender as the pink clouds. In the very garden where "Clementine in the Kitchen"* found her elusive snails, we have sipped an *apéritif* while

* Samuel Chamberlain, *Clementine in the Kitchen* (New York: Hastings House, rev. ed. 1963).

settling world problems with old friends in France, and then have eaten the best of real French onion soup prepared lovingly by the hostess herself in Clementine's old kitchen. We have warmed to hot porridge in the icy dining room of a hunting inn on the moors of Scotland; and listened at dawn for the faint crackling of dry brush signifying a deer going for a drink on the shore of a mountain lake in Oregon. Often we have picnicked at midday in the shade of trees in other romantic places, tasting the local breads, the wine and cheese and fresh fruit of the countryside.

Sometimes we have shared with hungry bees the sweet honey and jam we spread on brioches in the garden of an ancient Italian monastery, now a comfortable hotel high on a hill overlooking our favorite Italian city, Florence. While sitting at table beside an English country fireside, we have relished that purely English dessert, Trifle. And as we swung in a tiny cable-lift across the glaciers of Mont Blanc, we have shared our luncheon sandwiches with total strangers, gazing with awe and wonder at a corner of three great Alpine countries.

We can now picture with certainty that coffee-making ceremony at the crack of dawn at Camp Jane, ten thousand feet high in the Wind River Mountains of Wyoming, where old friend Theron Wasson, who discovered and named the site, catches fresh trout for breakfast and makes the coffee over his campfire with the icy water of Jakey's Fork. The coffee is the better for his skill and for the altitude and the keen mountain air. It could scarcely be duplicated in any other place—except in the White Mountains of New Hampshire on a September morning. Theron carries mocha-java beans in his pack and grinds the coffee he needs for a six-cup black enamelware pot. Into the pot go four cups of the mountain water, then four rounded tablespoons of ground coffee. The coffee is brought to a simmering boil over the campfire, then about a third of a cup of cold water is poured in. The pot is put beside the fire to settle and to keep hot. At this high altitude the coffee boils at 195 degrees, a factor which Theron declares makes unsurpassable coffee. A pinch of salt put in with the ground coffee improves the flavor, he believes. Just thinking about it evokes the fragrance of the spruce trees, the tingle of pure early morning mountain air, the taste of the delicious mountain-brook coffee.

Judging from the numbers of camping trailers on the roads across the country, all of America has become itinerant during the fine seasons, and it behooves all campers to know how to make fine coffee over a campfire, warming and flavorful.

We enjoy travels in three stages. The anticipation and the planning are full of dreams and eagerness; the reality is glamorous and exciting; the memory is a priceless treasure. Even so simple a journey as a picnic on the riverbank can be memorable in these three ways.

The Septembers we remember with the most fondness, in spite of all the glamour of the faraway places, are the ones when we stay close to our own dooryard. Freed from garden and other cares, we can explore the shunpikes of New England, none of them more than a day's journey from home. We can go to the fairs, spend a day or two antiquing. There can be a day for picking cranberries and one for beach plums. We can join a neighbor's quilting bee or have one of our own. We can go to the beach for a lobster picnic, picking up driftwood along the quiet beaches, and gathering shells for the garden borders.

We have time in September to watch the chipmunks with bulging cheeks scurry into the stone walls; and to admire the hummingbirds, still busy among the fuchsias and geraniums. We have time to pick mushrooms down the lane and in the old orchard where the boughs now bend with ripening fruit. Our trees are old and gnarled and widely scattered. We sometimes think they look as if they had been planted by Johnny Appleseed's wide-flung arms. Johnny Appleseed was a wandering New Englander, whose concern for his fellow man prompted him to scatter apple seeds as far away as his feet could find paths to follow.

Let all unselfish spirits heed
The story of Johnny Appleseed.
He had another and prouder name
In far New England, whence he came,
But by this title, and this alone,
Was the kindly wanderer loved and known.

—ELIZABETH AKERS ALLEN

Johnny Appleseed's "prouder name" was John Chapman. He was born in Leominster, Massachusetts, on September 26, 1774. He died a beloved character many years later, in 1847, a man of benevolent eccentricity and wanderlust.

And there was "The Old Darned Man" who was indeed darned and patched as he shuffled along the back roads of New England searching for the bride who failed to join him at the altar. He wore his black wedding suit to the day of his death in the hope that when at last he found her, he could take her by the hand and lead her to the church for those vows she did not take. From house to house he asked for her, doing chores for his board, staying but a night wherever warmhearted people invited him in. And he relied, too, on these kind people to darn the holes and brush the dust from his best black suit, until at last The Old Darned Man, as he was affectionately known to everyone, could search no more.

Another vagabond, New England-born Rufus Porter, left his special mark in many a beautiful old house where he painted the walls with scenes he remembered from his journeys, using colors he mixed himself. Some of these paintings exist today, one hundred and fifty years later, in those old homes. We have had time to explore some of them on a day in September.

New England abounds in exhibits of handwork done in earlier times as well as the present. Ours is a proud heritage of skill and good taste now being appreciated more deeply. Many with deft fingers are now following the example of our forebears, taking pride in their crewelwork, their hooked and braided rugs, their fine weaving, hand-turned pottery, and their samplers. The handwork of the Saffron and Indigo Society is as splendid as their colorful name. There is a Society of Blue and White, which surely must dye and spin and weave the coverlets for their own four-poster beds. There is a Needle and Bobbin Club, whose activities are apparent in the name. September is the month to call the first fall meeting of these busy groups and to thread looms, needles, and bobbins.

On a rainy September day, we go up to the rafter room and look into the chest where old quilts are kept, and wonder if we should start piecing another one. Here is the Tulip quilt, pieced and quilted by my mother's skilled hands. There is the Queen Charlotte's Crown quilt, Martha Washington's Flower Garden, Rose of Sharon. Log Cabin pattern is done in colorful cotton, and another is done in old silks, with featherstitching along the edges.

Patchwork quilts are one of the real American crafts. They were a practical way to use up the smallest scraps of cotton and silk material, as the hooked and braided rugs used woolens. At first the quilts were more utilitarian than beautiful, but gradually artistic designs and patterns and colors were employed and quilts became heirloom pieces of handwork. American ladies were sociable people, and soon it was discovered that many hands made light work. The Quilting Bee brought together neighbors and friends who could gossip and exchange appetizing receipts and enjoy a good hearty midday dinner and finish a quilt in no time at all. The best quilters could tuck their fine sharp short needles in and out eight times to an inch while discussing the latest village scandal. The beautiful quilts they fashioned in this sociable way are treasured today by anyone who owns one.

In my work basket there is a pillow of crewelwork, half-done since last winter; it is finished in a couple of September evenings by the fireside. Real crewel yarn is a joy to use. It is strong and durable, a fine-twisted wool from long fibers, hand-dyed with vegetables or bark or lichens or weeds. The stitches employed are simple but varied. I can do them in my sleep—lazy-daisy stitch, the buttonhole, satin, long and short, outline, chain, French-knot stitches. The trick is to do them evenly and in the proper places to get the right effect of light and shadow. In colonial America, ladies often copied English patterns, which in turn were based on the colorful motifs of East Indian origin. Hand-woven linen in natural colors was the base. Some of the best and most beautiful American work, however, was in original patterns which were simpler than those of the English, and so much better suited to our simpler way of life. To save hard-to-come-by yarns, there was devised the thrifty "New England stitch" which filled in designs without wasting thread on the back of the canvas where it didn't show.

Most little girls in colonial times were taught to do these stitches by means of samplers which hang on the walls of many New England homes and museums today. They are delightful examples of the disciplined skill of each pair of hands, made to do a stint every day. Such samplers were often done in simple cross-stitch on hand-woven linen which was probably produced at the family hearthside. They might have been designed by the little girls themselves, with the help of their mothers or their teachers, and one finds houses, dogs, cats, horses, flowers, trees, and sometimes even people embroidered around the edges. In the center of the sampler was usually stitched the alphabet and the numbers, a verse, and the name of the child, perhaps even the date of completion or her age.

Among our treasures is the smallest sampler we have ever seen, made by an ancestress named Eliza Johnson, dated October 18, 1827. Eliza was born in 1809, so she was eighteen when she completed her sampler, older perhaps than many who made them, but it seems improbable that a younger child could have done such fine stitching on a piece of linen of handkerchief texture. The wee sampler measures 2¼ inches by 3 inches, and is encased in a narrow, black-lacquered frame. It contains an alphabet of Old English capital letters one-quarter of an inch high; then the numbers; another alphabet of smaller letters; and to finish out the last row another group of numbers. There follows her name, then the date. Between each row of letters are tiny cross-stitch motifs, each line different in design. With this sampler we treasure a daguerreotype of Miss Eliza as a middle-aged woman, her countenance stern, her long graceful fingers holding a crocheted reticule which she undoubtedly made herself. Miss Eliza never married. Her face displays no joy or pleasure in life. Somehow I think she would be pleased if she knew how much her little sampler is treasured.

In an old sewing box we found another sampler which we keep because it amuses us. It was done by Polly Tenny, who is no kin of ours, although the sewing box belonged to a great-aunt. Polly was not as skilled as Miss Eliza Johnson. Her sampler looks something like this:

```
A   B   C   D   E   F   G   H   I   J   K   L
M   N   O   P   Q   R   S   T   U   *   *   V
W   X   Y   Z   *           P   O   *   *   L
Y   *   T   E   N   N   *   Y   *   ISM  Y
N   A   M   E   A   N   D   W   I   T  HMY
N   E   E   D   L   E   *   I   W   R  OUG
HTT II  E   S   A   M   E  I FMY  SKI
L   L   H   A   D   B  EEN  B   E  T  T
```

But her skill wasn't better and the sampler wasn't finished for Polly had run out of room. The colors of cotton thread used are now faded red, black, and yellow, but some of the letters were done in light-blue silk which is still as bright as when it was stitched into the linen. Was Polly a tomboy who hated sitting on a cushion sewing a fine seam? Did she grow up to be someone who did not need to use a needle—an actress or a musician or a dancing teacher? We hope so.

A New England September is one of the most precious months of the year. Fat tomatoes ripen on the vines and fall lettuce is crisp and green. Cucumbers and squash and cabbages and sweet corn are better from our own garden than any other.

Home from our wanderings, I put on my apron again and try to reconstruct some of the delectable dishes we have eaten in England or France or Austria; or Connecticut, Rhode Island, Massachusetts, Vermont, Maine, and New Hampshire. We sort over the cranberries we have picked in our secret bog within five miles of home; peel tree-ripe crisp sweet apples; dream up a raspberry soufflé, also "tender as the pink clouds over the Mediterranean"; make an English Trifle using plump raspberries from the last picking of everbearings. It's good to be home in September.

CRANBERRY-APPLE CRISP

2 cups fresh cranberries
3 cups coarsely diced peeled
    apples
1 cup white sugar
1½ cup rolled oats

¾ cup maple syrup
½ cup butter
½ tsp. salt
Fresh-grated nutmeg

Butter generously a baking dish. Pour the cranberries, apples, and white sugar into it and mix them together. In a bowl mix the rolled oats, butter, and salt, add the maple syrup and pour over the fruit in the baking dish. Grate nutmeg over the top. Bake at 350° for about 1 hour or until cranberries and apples are tender and the top is browned. One cup of brown sugar may be used in place of the maple syrup.

CRANBERRY-APPLE PIE

½ cup sugar	½ cup honey
2 Tbs. flour	2 Tbs. butter
¼ tsp. salt	2 cups fresh cranberries
¼ tsp. cinnamon	2 cups peeled sliced apples
Grated rind of one orange	Dash of grated nutmeg

Pastry for a 2-crust pie

In a large saucepan combine sugar, flour, seasonings, orange peel, honey, and butter. Bring to a boil and cook for 2 minutes, stirring until sugar has dissolved and mixture is well blended. Add cranberries and apples to the mixture, bring to a boil again, and cook until cranberries have popped. Cool this mixture.

Make pastry and line a 9-inch pie plate with half the rolled pastry, leaving crust to extend 1 inch over edge of plate; trim. Pour the cooled mixture into the pastry-lined pan, dust with nutmeg. Cover with strips of pastry woven in lattice fashion. Fold bottom edges up over ends of lattice strips and flute edge. Bake at 425° for 15 minutes; reduce heat to 375° and bake another 20–25 minutes until browned and bubbly.

RASPBERRY TRIFLE

Split 11 ladyfingers (may be homemade or boughten) and arrange the halves on the bottom and around the sides of a pretty glass dish. Crumble 1 ladyfinger on the bottom, loosely filling in the spaces between ladyfingers. Sprinkle the cake with ⅓ cup of good sherry. Pour custard (receipt follows) into the dish on top of ladyfingers.

For the custard, beat well 4 egg yolks. In a saucepan, stir together ½ cup sugar, 2 Tbs. cornstarch, and ¼ tsp. salt. Add 2½ cups milk and cook and stir until the mixture comes to a boil. Stir vigorously and boil for 1 minute and remove from heat. Spoon a little of this mixture into the beaten egg

yolks and blend well, then pour the yolk mixture into the saucepan, and
bring again just to the boil while stirring. Cool a little in the pan, then add
1 Tbs. vanilla. Pour this mixture over the ladyfingers. Cool in refrigerator
until well set.

When ready to serve, pour 1 cup of fresh or thawed frozen raspberries,
slightly sweetened, over the custard, and garnish with sweetened whipped
cream, chopped blanched almonds, and small pieces of candied angelica
(see p. 144).

RASPBERRY SOUFFLÉ BEAULIEU

3 Tbs. butter	2 Tbs. raspberry cordial
3 Tbs. flour	3 egg yolks
1 cup milk	5 egg whites
½ cup sugar	

Butter and sugar the bottom and sides of a 1½-quart soufflé dish. Make
a thick white sauce of the butter, flour, milk, and sugar. Beat egg yolks until
thick, add slowly to white sauce while stirring. Remove from fire. Beat whites
until stiff, fold the white sauce into them slowly. Pour into soufflé dish. Bake
at 350° until high and well browned. Serve with raspberry sauce. I hope you
have an oven with a glass door, for one should not be tempted to peek until
the soufflé is done. It generally takes about 40 minutes.

RASPBERRY SAUCE

⅓ cup sugar	1½ to 2 cups fresh or thawed
⅓ cup water	frozen raspberries
1 Tbs. cornstarch	

Boil and stir all ingredients together until thick and smooth, about
3 minutes. Strain through a sieve and serve warm in silver sauce tureen,

with ¼ cup flaming brandy atop. This sauce is also delicious poured over canned pear halves, pound cake, or vanilla ice cream.

Old roads winding as old roads will,
Here to a ferry, and there to a mill,
And glimpses of chimneys and gabled eaves
Through green elm arches and maple leaves.
—JOHN GREENLEAF WHITTIER

Portrait—Rufus Porter

A ROLLING STONE

HE WAS many years ahead of his time. Rufus Porter was born in West Boxford, Massachusetts, in 1792 and for ninety-three years he wove in and out of New England towns and villages fiddling, teaching, inventing, painting, writing, always with a restless urge to keep busy and be productive and to wander.

He was the son of a prosperous farmer whose gentle, industrious family had for generations tilled their farm contentedly. But the founding of the new democracy had brought a new confidence to its people. There stirred in many a New England breast a desire to explore other horizons. The Porters of West Boxford, typifying this restlessness, pulled up stakes and moved to the near-wilderness area of Maine to seek new fortunes and ways of life. Their son Rufus was to go even farther afield, living a long life of variety, adventure, and freedom, leaving a trail of talented accomplishments across New England.

His formal schooling lasted only a few months, but this eager young man was filled with an urgency to learn by his own methods and in his own way. For a time his father apprenticed him to a shoemaker, hoping the boy would settle down to a respectable trade, but this tap-tapping was much too humdrum for so spirited a lad, and so at the early age of fifteen he put his fife and his fiddle under his arm and began a life of wandering. He played for military drills and gay dancing parties wherever he could. And when he had learned all he thought there was to know about his musical instruments, he wrote books about them, teaching his knowledge to others.

Before long, he had turned from fiddling to house-painting. In those days a painter had to know how to grind and mix his own paints and make his own brushes, and how to use paints in decorating plastered walls, woodwork, furniture, and signs, as well as the exterior of buildings.

Young Porter apparently found his new career an interesting one to which he could apply his inventive, inquisitive mind. He also enjoyed the freedom it allowed him to move about at will from place to place, as other itinerant painters of the time were doing, hardly staying in any one spot long enough to have a home.

He acquired a family, however, for in 1815 he married Miss Eunice Twombly of Portland, Maine, and in eighteen years there were ten children. It is doubtful that his family followed in his wandering footsteps, and it is also doubtful that he felt any obligation to be a very permanent part of the household, for he continued to travel about. His wife died after thirty-three years of this unsettled kind of home life, and the following year Mr. Porter was married again, in Brooklyn, New York. Six children were born to this second union, only one of which survived infancy. With a total of sixteen offspring, it would seem that Rufus Porter did find it convenient to return "home" occasionally from his footloose traveling.

He pursued a career of painting for many years. Among the techniques he acquired was one called "graining" which was a way of simulating with paints the grain of wood. This technique was applied to woodwork and paneling in houses, on furniture and chests. Stenciling was another technique he learned, in which he applied paint or powder through cut stencils onto tacky varnish, often using as a brush his finger wrapped in velvet to give a soft effect. Sometimes he used a cork or a sponge for his effects on wood or plaster. With these devices he decorated sleighs, drums, boxes, mirrors, and furniture, as well as walls and woodwork.

For a time he cut profiles (silhouettes) and painted small portraits, putting them in frames and selling them for a few cents each. Some of his work was signed, much of it was not. In most cases, he became so proficient in his craft that he turned to teaching and writing instruction books, thus adding to his income and his enjoyment of his work.

All of this time, the artist was traveling throughout New England and going as far south as Virginia, even venturing by ship to the West Coast and to Hawaii. Generally he earned his board and room by painting, and he was especially clever at decorating the walls of homes or taverns where he stayed. It is by this painting of murals that he is chiefly known today. His frescoes were freehand, imaginative, and colorful. All across New England in old houses today a search is being conducted for remnants of his painted murals, but many have succumbed to the changes of the years and have been destroyed.

These murals are now considered to be among the most important artistic contributions of their time, limned by an especially imaginative genius. The landscapes which he so charmingly painted were scenes Porter had remembered all his life, from military drills to farmscapes, from romantic waterfalls to woodland scenes, from rocks and mountains to the sea and ships, and even a volcano reminiscent of his Hawaiian adventure. He had a special trick of tailoring his wall paintings to fit the available space, even managing his waterfalls and mountains along stair wainscotings to give an effect of height.

As Porter grew older, he grew increasingly interested in many other phases of nineteenth-century American life. He became a prolific inventor of mechanical contrivances which were so far ahead of his time that his ideas were scorned: a washing machine; a dryer; what was probably the first mobile home—a portable house containing five rooms which he said was warm and comfortable; an alarm clock; an automobile; an airship; a hot-air ventilating system. He had considerable faith in his inventions and founded several scientific magazines to publicize them and other advancements of the time, doing most of the writing himself.

Such an inventive and clever man should have been highly successful but to tell the truth no one had enough confidence to help him test, finance, or market his ideas, although many of them were the forerunners of things in use today. At a time when industry was expanding rapidly, he was using his creative ability to find schemes which would save labor and time in the home, on the farm, in the factory, even in the air. His ideas were generally rational and practical, but just too advanced.

He was unfortunately so impractical and casual about patenting and marketing his devices that he was not given credit nor appropriate financial reward, nor did he have the satisfaction which might have come from realizing that he was one of the great American inventors.

This clever, talented, footloose, and carefree man of the nineteenth century, who seemed especially to enjoy painting on the walls of pleasant houses the scenes of farms which showed an abundant, thrifty, happy, orderly life, never lived the kind of life he portrayed. He died at the age of ninety-three, unappreciated and unmourned. Only now, one hundred years later, is his work being proclaimed, and coveted. Perhaps his life was led for the special purpose of proving the truth of the old, old adage—a rolling stone gathers no moss.

> September—
> The beautiful apples, so golden and mellow
>   They will fall at a kiss of the breeze,
> While it breathes through the foliage frosty and
>   yellow
> And the sunshine is filling the trees!
>   —JOHN JAMES PIATT

OCTOBER

Birthstone and Birthdays

The Birthstone for October is the *Opal*, for *Hope*.

1	16
2	17
3	18
4	19
5	20
6	21
7	22
8	23
9	24
10	25
11	26
12	27
13	28
14	29
15	30
	31

Flower

THE MARIGOLD
Tagetes

NO BRIGHTER picture can be painted in the dooryard than that produced by plantings of some member of the Marigold clan. In gay colors of yellow and orange and brown, they are best when planted in rows or masses. Some varieties are dwarf and make fine edgings in a green and yellow garden, or around the herb garden.

In Great-Grandmother's day, the Marigold was cultivated as it had been for several centuries as a medicinal herb ("a comforter of heart and spirits," remarked Dr. Culpeper) and it was also believed that a planting of Marigolds rid the soil and neighboring plants of insects. This claimed virtue has been authenticated to some degree by the recent discovery and testing of their efficacy in this regard—Marigolds do indeed rid the soil of nematodes, a tiny worm which feeds on the roots of plants, and they remain thus effective in the garden for at least three years after being planted.

The Marigold is a native of Central and South America. It flourishes as an annual in New England gardens, blooming from July until frost. When being used for flower arrangements, it is best to strip off all the lower leaves which might be under water, as they soon become overpungent and many people object to the odor. Many new varieties have been hybridized, producing plants from the miniature size to giants, and in many strikingly vivid colors of the yellow and brown hues. They are perfectly happy in average to poor soil, and like bright sunshine all day long.

The calendula, sometimes called pot-marigold, is not a true Marigold but is a cousin also belonging to the Composite family of flowers, those which might be under water, as they soon become overpungent and many lion, joe-pye weed, aster, goldenrod, ragweed, daisy, coneflower and sunflower, coreopsis, tansy, wormwood, everlasting, thistle, hawkweed, lettuce, and some others.

In the language of flowers, Marigold meant Jealousy, for reasons known only to those who compiled the language.

> Open afresh your round of starry folds,
> Ye ardent marigolds!
> —JOHN KEATS, "I Stood Tip-Toe"

Solution of the problem concerning the orchard of nineteen trees, on page 154:

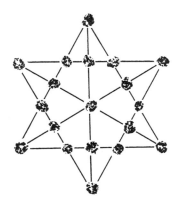

Bird

THE PHOEBE
Sayornis phoebe

A Phoebe makes a little print
Upon the floors of Fame.
—EMILY DICKINSON

WERE the Phoebe the only bird in the dooryard, he would be beloved indeed, for there is nothing but good to be said of him. His lack of fame is due to the fact that he lives his life in such quiet repose, going about his own business with no fuss, no bother, no excitement so that one scarcely knows he is around. He loves his wife (being mated to her for life) and his family, builds his house with care and artistry, pays his taxes and contributes to the welfare of the community in which he lives by consuming myriad troublesome flying insects. He asks nothing of us except to be left alone and he is an excellent neighbor. He is the best of birds.

This neatly garbed vicar of the garden has christened himself. He repeats his own name over and over again as he goes about his daily tasks, saying "Phee-bee" quite articulately as he perches on the limb of a tree, on the back of the garden bench or chair, or on the tip of the clothes pole. From these open perches, he watches for the flying insects which constitute almost his only food in the summer. He will suddenly dart into the air and with a sharp click of his beak snap up an insect which he sees, sometimes several of them in succession, maneuvering skillfully on the wing as he does so. Then he will return to his perch and watch for another tidbit. He is a tireless hunter and so dexterous as to be sure of catching any insect in the air on which he sets his mind.

The Phoebe is one of the flycatcher clan, members of which are rather undistinguished as to dress, but are valuable for their insect-eating proclivities. He is about seven inches long, larger than the peewee, a cousin with whom he is often confused. He has a habit of waving his tail up and down (and sometimes flicking it sideways) which also distinguishes him from his relatives. His call is more emphatic than that of the peewee, or of the chickadee (no relation), which whistles the same kind of notes. His voice is expressive, musical, and pleasant to hear.

Early in the spring, the Phoebes come north, the male arriving first. He inspects the year's building sites, and mopes around a bit until his wife arrives a few days later. There is a happy reunion and the nest-building begins very soon. Once they have found a good location, they will build there year after year or if it becomes necessary to move, they will try to find another place very near. They may or may not use the same nest if it is still in existence, even in the same year, for successive broods. But because they sometimes will make use of an old nest, it is wise to help them after the first brood has left it by removing the old nest and lightly spraying the area with a nontoxic insect spray if possible, as their habit of using hen feathers for the nest lining can infest the nest with lice so injurious to the newly hatched birds.

Phoebes are adobe builders, having been cliff-dwellers before the age of man-made barns. But they are smarter than many of the birds who build their nests with mud, such as robins, for they seem to realize that a heavy rainstorm can soften such nests to the point of disintegration. So the Phoebe builds his house in a place sheltered from rain—inside open porches, henhouses, barns, sheds, under gables or the frames of bridges. The nest is made of moss and lichens well plastered together with mud and lined with fine grass, feathers, or hair. It is a pretty nest, the moss and lichens giving it a color and texture almost of stonework.

These gentle birds dearly love a woodland retreat near the water where flying insects abound. In such places, they will often build in the high banks of streams much in the way their ancestors built in cliffs. Or if a bridge is available, they find a cozy spot protected from the weather, the old covered bridges being particularly enticing. They are in fact called "bridge birds" by old-fashioned New Englanders, a delightful and appropriate name. We have often picnicked or fished for trout beneath a covered bridge, accompanied by the Phoebes who lived beneath the timbers.

The nests are four- to five-inch cups, in which there are usually laid five or six white eggs. Since the Phoebe comes to New England very early and stays so late in the fall, there will always be two broods and sometimes three in a season. In some sections they can be found all winter, at which time their diet must become largely vegetarian. When they do migrate in October, they travel south to an area from the Carolinas to Mexico, Central America, and the West Indies.

Phoebes find convenient lunching and bathing spots in our West Field with its little pools of rainwater and its myriad insects. All day as we go about the garden doing our chores there, the Phoebe follows us, a happy companion who tells us his name over and over, his claim to fame. If he didn't tell us who he was, we might not notice this plain little bird with the olive-gray back and gray breast, the vicar of the garden.

O birds, your perfect virtues bring,
Your song, your forms, your rhythmic flight,
Your manners for the heart's delight,
Nestle in hedge, or barn, or roof,
Here weave your chamber weatherproof.

—RALPH WALDO EMERSON

This Treasure Chest of Old Beams

O suns and skies and clouds of June,
And flowers of June together,
Ye cannot rival for one hour
October's bright blue weather.
—HELEN HUNT JACKSON

IT IS the Indians' Moon of the Falling Leaf. Flaming colors like the brightest fruits enrich the hills: orange, tangerine, lemon, russet and damson purple, lime and avocado. Vines of bittersweet and turquoise berries festoon the stone walls down the lane in garlands of color; wild clematis wear bonnets of fairy feathers.

The smell of autumn is in the earth, in the ripe apples and new cider, in the bayberry and wet grass and bracken, in the clean sea and the clear pure air. Country roads wander deep in banks of fern and wear soft blankets the color of fallen leaves. Clean-trimmed stone walls and weathered fences bind the fields with granite-gray braids.

Cold and as deliciously fragrant as a glass of champagne, the mornings glisten as the sun falls across fields silver with frost. A full golden flood illuminates the garden from the warm October sun which washes over maple and birch and oak leaves and touches the blossoms of witch hazel and chrysanthemum. We swish through dry leaves on the lawn and we rake, and rake, and rake. What harvest for the compost pile; what dividends in fine leaf mold in spring, bright flowers in summer.

The moon is full and as the frost creeps into the fields, we take an evening walk down the lane. In the distance a dog howls. Our own dog answers softly, follows close at our heels. Cassiopeia is spilling into the top of the big maple tree. Leaves drop in whispers. Behind us there is the snap of a twig which is not timed to our own footsteps; an acorn falls with a bounce on twig and branch and ground. There is a sudden soft burst of clapping hands—just the poplar leaves ("popple" leaves, the old-timers call them) rustling in the night wind. A pair of eyes gleams in the darkness ahead, and disappears silently into the stone wall—a fox? cat? weasel? Steddey sniffs anxiously, but at our word waits in obedience, as we suspect a skunk. We are conscious of tension and a strained listening. An owl's wings flap in the ancient pine trees and we stop in surprise at the unaccustomed sound. We take a step and are caught in the web of a spider.

In October the woods are haunted. The creaking limbs, the wind-stirred leaves, the snapping twigs, the falling acorns, the webs of spiders are the works of the Little People of the Woods. A rabbit runs ahead of us in the moonlight in panic, Steddy in brief pursuit. We remember that witches were once said to turn themselves into hares, the better to work their evil spells.

Ah, the woods are haunted in October by the same Little People who inhabit them every other month of the year. Thoughts of witches and goblins and elves in October have filled the world with fright longer than anyone can record with certainty, and the season would not be complete without this association. But "to him who in the love of Nature holds communion with her visible forms, she speaks a various language," sometimes with a slight accent of witchery, 'tis true.

Old houses where men and women and children have lived and loved and died are haunted, too. Do you know the spirit of an old house? Have you met any of the ghosts who inhabit an old house? Have you heard the voices that speak from the walls of an old house?

In its spirit there is a magic of tranquillity, a repose and a graciousness from the love that planned and protected and cherished it through the years.

Its ghosts are the influences of all those who have gone before, stronger than those who now dwell there, although one day they, too, will leave behind traces of themselves. The voices that speak from the walls may tell of the planning of a great revolution, of the sound of fifes or bugles as men went to wars; they may tell of laughter and song as joy filled their hearts; they may tell of soft weeping as sickness or death touched those who once lived there.

In the strong scent of its old wood, there is the perfume of lost forests. In the granite foundations set so firmly into the earth, there is lodged the strength of a now-vanished pioneer hope and determination. In the blackened fireplaces there is the warmth of many a bitter winter's night; the comfort of good meals for hungry families. The small-paned windows reflect peace and harmony and labor of all the lives that have dwelt there before. An old house preserves these things in every wall, every room, in every smooth-worn floorboard, every planed and beveled panel. An old house preserves the very history of our country.

It is a temptation to think that by our restoration and labor we have created the charm and character of our house ourselves; but in fact everything here has been given to us by those who have come before. Their spirits are surely here. Their candles first lighted the way from room to room; their lanterns guided the way from the ancient roadway which goes through the dooryard. Their unwritten bequest to us was this treasure chest of old beams and boards and bricks and glass—and the omen of good luck which comes from finding the original crane still hanging in the old fireplace.

Sometimes in imagining the past of the house, the present fades and the people and things all around vanish. Sometimes I have looked into the fire-light in our Old Kitchen and for a moment have felt the real presence of another person, unseen. Sometimes the slow ticking of the grandfather clock recalls the scene when the first clock in our town was placed in the very corner where this pendulum now swings in a quiet rhythm. What excitement there must have been in the family and in the town as the neighbors came to see, to touch, and to hear the clear strike of hours of the only clock in town.

The furniture in our house has all come from other old houses including those of some of our ancestors. The pieces dwell here with us in perfect peace with the paneled and plastered walls under the low ceilings. Even such inanimate objects as these represent once-living beings. In a chest or table or chair is the skill of a carpenter or cabinetmaker whose tools did his bidding to create a thing of grace and utility. In the coverlets are the skill of past weavers whose deft fingers spun the wool, wound the warp, and threaded and wove it with measured precision. In the braided, hooked, and woven rugs on the floor are the thrift and imagination of wives whose households were run in strictest though cheerful economy. Even the wrought-iron doorknocker made by our old blacksmith neighbor echoes the blows on his anvil.

In the red wagon seat now serving a useful purpose in the hall is there a story of a pretty girl going to a country dance? A family going to Meeting? Boys and girls going sleighing or skating? A farmer and his wife taking their harvest to market? . . . A pewter teapot on the mantel we know was the only piece of pewter left when its long-gone owner carried his household store of pewterware to the blacksmith to be melted and made into bullets in a distant wartime, a sacrifice for any American householder. . . . Can you picture the scene by the fireside as Great-Grandmother's tea caddy with its little silver caddy-spoon was unlocked to brew a pot of tea for her guest?

In quiet good manners, our house has accepted, even welcomed, our presence here, perhaps because it senses our love for it. But we have been amused to find that to others less understanding of its characteristics the house sometimes shows aloofness and inhospitality. While some visitors have had no real suspicion of spirits that lurk about them, they have looked uneasy at times. A door which we know to sag a bit after two hundred years of swinging on its hand-wrought hinges will stick with obstinate strength for one who pulls impatiently to open it; a draft will blow across the shoulders of one who does not understand the need of a blazing hearthfire for air. Let one who does not love or understand an old house stay alone there for even a little while and he will hear noises which disturb and startle him. A thumb-latch will drop minutes after it has been lifted, filling the stillness with an ominous noise. Clapboards cooling off after a day in the sunshine will pop with a sharp snap. A chipmunk or squirrel running over the roof will sound like a hundred hooves racing. The branch of a bush scratching, scraping in a soft breeze against the clapboards, could be footsteps in the next room. The whine of a wasp caught in a spider web might be the voices of witches casting an evil spell. A shutter bangs in the wind, swallows flutter, or the wind whistles in the chimney. The teakettle boils over with a hiss and sputter, and the tea tastes bitter. The fireplace smokes; a bat squeaks in the night.

The ghosts of an old house can frighten him who lacks affinity; then chuckling, slip away into the deep shadowy night leaving to those of us who live here the joys of the warm hearthfire, the friendly soothing tick of the old clock, the tranquillity of the great rooms. So, if you do not know or love an old house, beware, for it's sure that on an October night

> The Gobble-uns'll git you
> Ef you
> Don't
> Watch
> Out!

A favorite actress and comedienne used to sing a song about the fairies at the bottom of the garden which amused us tremendously. There *are* fairies at the bottom of the garden, and we have often found their traces there. If you do not believe in fairies in the garden you are not a true gardener. They touch a box with a wand and make of it a palace for a homeless bird. In mischievous play, they pull up flowers and plant them in other more surprising places. They weave silken webs from flower to flower and paint the wings of butterflies. In October they blow on the bittersweet and make the berries pop open into gay necklaces of red and gold.

At midnight on the full of the October moon, the fairies harness a pumpkin to their coach-dog (who just happens to be our corgi Steddey Alexander) and go for a ride across fields and woods and mountains to some secret rendezvous with their Queen. If you don't believe this, look at the harness marks he (or any corgi) carries on his chest and back. He returns from such a midnight journey smiling widely and smelling of sweet grass and herbs. Since the eleventh century in Old Wales, corgis have been coach-dogs for the Fairy Queen. Any true Welshman will tell you so.

At the bottom of an old-fashioned garden the fairies arrange their mushroom conference stools in a fairy ring, and name all the flowers. Who else could have thought up such delightful names: sweet William, foxglove, basket of gold, snow in summer, feverfew and cowslip, johnny-jump-up or ladies' delight, Quaker ladies, ladies' tresses, trailing arbutus, hollyhocks, bouncing bet, sweet alyssum, love-lies-bleeding, bee-balm, larkspur, snapdragon, Star-of-Bethlehem, sweet rocket, honeysuckle, columbine, everlasting, thyme, honesty, poppy and Peter's wreath, satin-flower or money-in-both-pockets, virgin's bower, baby's breath and bachelor's buttons, morning glory and bleeding-heart. These fairy names retreat centuries into the dim and enchanted past of gardening.

When the fairies have opened the last roses, we go to the bottom of the garden and gather them to arrange in a crystal bowl. In all their enchanting colors, they blend from purest white and softest pink through salmon and yellow and golden orange to deepest red. We cut the sprays of bittersweet, now stripped of leaves, to arrange with pine cones and ground cedar in an old cheese basket, and hang it on the brown pine wall of the Old Kitchen. As a welcome on the doors, we hang old hand-wrought corn-dryers with colorful Indian corn, bittersweet, and pine. We plant the daffodil and tulip bulbs and push in the markers firmly, wondering if the fairies will rearrange them as they did last year so that daffodil John Evelyn becomes tulip Princess Elizabeth.

> There is a world in which we dwell,
> And yet a world invisible!
> And do not think that naught can be,
> Save only what with eyes ye see;
> I tell ye, that, this very hour,
> Had but your sight a spirit's power,
> Ye would be looking, eye to eye,
> At a terrific company!
> —HELEN PHILBROOK PATTEN

The pumpkins are stacked and two with wry faces and glaring eyes are lighted on the front door-rock each evening. Pumpkins were a staple food for early Americans, who inherited the vegetable from the Indians, and learned many ways to cook it from the Indians, too. In those days, pumpkin was cut in small pieces, strung on cords and hung before the fireplace to dry, then stored for year-round use. Everything was made of pumpkin, from beverages to soup, from pie to bread, from custard to cake, and even a kind of flour. The pioneers often wearied of their diet of pumpkin, but they were saved from starvation in many a lean, cold winter.

Though rich in color, pumpkin is rather bland in taste and so we add spices or herbs to it for additional flavor. Our favorite pumpkin dish is chiffon pie, but custard, fritters, and cookies are close seconds. On Hallowe'en we have a big basket of pumpkin cookies waiting for trick-or-treat callers; and the pie, custard, and fritters are good company fare any other day.

PUMPKIN CHIFFON PIE

Prepare a 9-inch *baked* pie shell.
Soak 1 envelope gelatin in ¼ cup cold water.
In a double boiler, beat 3 egg yolks and add:

½ cup brown sugar	¼ tsp. each salt and ginger
1¼ cups canned or cooked pumpkin purée	½ tsp. each cinnamon and nutmeg
½ cup milk	

Cook and stir over hot water until thick. Stir in the soaked gelatin until dissolved. Cool. Beat 3 egg whites and ¼ tsp. salt until stiff. When pumpkin mixture begins to set, stir in ½ cup sugar and fold in the egg whites. Fill the pie shell and chill for several hours. Garnish with whipped cream; if desired, shredded coconut or chopped nuts may be sprinkled on top of the pie before adding cream.

PUMPKIN COOKIES

½ cup soft (but not melted) butter	2½ cups flour
1¼ cups firmly packed brown sugar	1 Tbs. baking powder
2 well-beaten eggs	¼ tsp. ginger
1½ cups canned or cooked pumpkin	1 tsp. cinnamon
	½ tsp. each nutmeg and salt
	1½ cup chopped butternuts or black walnuts

Cream butter and sugar together until light. Mix in the beaten eggs and the pumpkin. Mix dry ingredients together and add to the pumpkin mixture and stir until batter is well blended. Add nut meats. Drop by tea-spoonfuls onto buttered baking sheet (half-teaspoonfuls make a good size for tea or dessert cookies). Bake in preheated 400° oven for 15 minutes until very lightly browned. Makes about 75 cookies.

PUMPKIN FRITTERS

2 eggs beaten light	½ cup milk
2 cups cooked or canned pumpkin	1 cup flour
Pinch of salt	2 tsp. baking powder
½ tsp. cinnamon	2 Tbs. sugar
¼ tsp. each nutmeg and ground cloves	

Mix ingredients together and drop by rounded teaspoonfuls in a kettle of deep fat heated to 375°. Cook until browned, turn and brown on the other side. Drain on paper towels. Dust with powdered sugar. May be eaten plain with a meat course. They are also delicious served with maple syrup for dessert or for breakfast.

PUMPKIN CUSTARD

Mix together:

2 cups cooked or canned pumpkin	1½ tsp. cinnamon
1 cup milk	1½ tsp. ginger
1 cup heavy cream	½ tsp. salt
½ cup maple syrup	¼ tsp. nutmeg
½ cup white sugar	4 well-beaten eggs
	1 Tbs. good brandy

Pour the mixture into a buttered 1½-quart soufflé dish (or 10 old-fashioned brown custard cups) and place dish in pan containing an inch of hot water. Bake at 325° for 50–60 minutes until knife inserted in center comes out clean (it may be moist, however). Let custard cool, then chill thoroughly for several hours. When ready to serve, run a knife around the edge of the dish to loosen custard. Invert onto serving plate. Serve with a garnish of whole pecans and sweetened whipped cream.

> What moistens the lip and what brightens the eye?
> What calls back the past like the rich Pumpkin pie?
> —JOHN GREENLEAF WHITTIER

Portrait—Sherman Pliny Fellows

THE VILLAGE BLACKSMITH

"I WAS born fifty years too late," the old blacksmith said sadly. "The automo*beel* doesn't have to be shod." He was sitting on the stone wall watching me hoe the asparagus bed, his large knotted hands curved over thin bony knees. "But Sherm," I protested, "if that is so you wouldn't have been here to make this good light hoe for me, or to mend my pump, or to make those fine andirons for the Old Kitchen fireplace." The old gentleman smiled and said gently, "Yes, I enjoyed doing those things, but it's shoeing hosses I was trained to do." And *wanted to do*, he might have added, for he loved animals and found satisfaction in their company which was natural to a country blacksmith and farmer.

Sherman Fellows and his wife Blanche were our nearest neighbors, and the first to greet us when we moved to the old farm many years ago. Their sincere warmth and friendliness belied the tales I had heard of New England country people and their reluctance to accept strangers as their own. As long as they lived, we were neighbors of mutual love and respect, and I miss them to this day, though they have both been gone a long time.

We took possession of the farm on the first day of June. Scarcely had we kindled a fire in the smoky old range on that cold rainy day and put the teakettle on, when the white-haired, clean-shaven gentleman came to the summer kitchen door to inquire if he and his wife could be of any help to us, at the same time handing in through the door a pan of fresh-from-the-oven rolls. At our invitation he came into the kitchen, where we had temporarily set up camp chairs and had scrubbed off an old bench to use as a table. We chatted there amiably for an hour or more while the kitchen and our friendship warmed together.

Yes, perhaps he could help, and we discussed cleaning out the stovepipe which wound itself up and into a hole chopped out of the old fireplace chimney. "Sure to stop the smoking," he agreed. "A good chimney fire might help, too. I always let a chimney fire burn itself out—gets rid of a lot of creosote in the chimney. Saves getting up on the roof with a bag of sand on a chain." We looked at each other in amazement and agreed later that we must have a lot to learn about country living. But when we saw Sherm starting his woodstove fires with kerosene, and drying his wood in the oven (which got too dry one day and caught fire), we thought there were some things a blacksmith long used to dealing with fire-building could do which we dared not try.

Sherman Pliny Fellows had been born in September 1868, in the little house next door to ours, and he was proud of having seen the first light of day in the very room where Dan'l Webster had been married to Miss Grace Fletcher many years before. He was equally proud of having gone to the same school that Dan'l (it is never pronounced any other way in New Hampshire) attended, and had in fact used the same school bench. The bench has long gone, but the little house and the Academy Building are still here.

Sherm's father and grandfather had gone West during the Gold Rush years. When his father, Pliny Fellows, returned after a long absence in the West (none the richer), he found still waiting for him the girl he had left behind, and so they were married and settled quietly into life in the village. Pliny built a little blacksmith shop across the street from his home, where he worked and taught his only son, Sherman, the trade of shoeing horses and oxen, and of working with iron. Mr. Pliny was a violin teacher and dancing master as well, and as late as a couple of years ago, his violin was still being played by a neighbor for country dances held in the Grange Hall, as the Academy has lately been called.

Sherman and Blanche moved into one of the nicest houses in town when an uncle who lived there died and his estate went to them. They were proud of its history, as the house had been well built for a minister of the church. But the original stenciling on many of the walls and the broad staircase rising from the central hall did not mean as much to them as the warm kitchen and the snug barn. They lived there comfortably and happily and simply for many years; only in their last years did the specter of want and sickness mar their life together.

Sherm was full of good stories. He told them with a wit and humor that he himself enjoyed. Often he would sit at our fireside and relate stories of his trading days, and would slap his knees with glee when he told of finally getting the better of a man who once had swapped him a nag which occasionally had fits (Sherm called it a "fitty hoss"). His father had once traded a grandfather clock for some seed potatoes, and figured he got the best of the bargain because the clock wouldn't run, and the potatoes produced a good crop.

On another day he told admiringly of how "Morgie" (Morgia) Webster, one of two sisters who ran large farms in the town, had fooled a slicker from downstate who had long been pestering her to sell a pair of oxen. One afternoon when the farmer came with what he said was a final offer, she invited him in to supper. There was plenty of strong cider on the table along with a good hot meal. She told him that at last she had a well-matched pair of fine oxen she might be persuaded to part with—not anxious to, of course, but if the price were right she did need a little money just then. The downstate farmer, now in an affable mood, went with her to the dimly lighted barn to look over the oxen. They made their deal with little delay, the farmer took away the oxen, and Morgie put the money out of reach. Only then did she and her trusted hired man chuckle together over their conspiracy to stage-dress the oxen, one of which was six inches or so shorter than the other. During supper when Morgie was being particularly solicitous that her guest be well fed and happy, the hired man had gone into the barn, put some thick planks on the floor under the short ox and covered them with hay. The downstate bargainer didn't know the difference until the next day, when it was too late.

"I mistrust there are some people might think this dishonest," said Sherm, watching me with interest. "But I knew that feller and he was aggravatin'. He was a liar. There's two kinds of men I do hate and despise, a liar and a thief. The thief an't so bad, you can put him in jail if you ketch him. But of the two I hate the liar the most—you can't do *nawthin'* about him." Then he added thoughtfully, "Course, you're not obliged to believe all he says."

A fire in the village called for the help of every man, and with so little protection against it, the possibility of a fire was a constant worry to everyone. Dirty and tired from fighting a particularly tragic fire which burned a fine house to the ground, Sherm afterward shook his head disapprovingly and said, "There's two kinds of fires—cigarettes and them that's set [for insurance money]." The possibility that a chimney fire could burn down an old house didn't seem to enter his mind.

Weather to the farmer in New England, as everywhere, is daily the most important conversation piece. Everything depends on it: his planting, his harvest for family and stock, his fishing days, his hunting success, even his disposition and health. Sherm was scornful of the weather predictions he read in the paper and heard on the radio. "I have only to look to the Mount'in [Mount Kearsarge] to tell what the weather will be, and I figure I do a better job of predictin' than they do." We used to trade weather sayings, and sometimes we made up verses from his predictions such as we saw printed in the Almanac which hung on our kitchen mantelpiece. Some of these simple verses were not bad, but some of them would send us all into gales of laughter. One that I particularly remember was sensible:

An out wind's a sign
Of wet clothes on the line.

An "out wind" to Sherm was an east wind from "out" in the Atlantic, and an east wind always brings moisture guaranteed to give an extra rinse to a wash hanging on the clothesline.

Yes, to Sherm the good old days were gone. He charged fifty cents for shoeing a horse, and when I recently heard that a busy blacksmith could get fifteen dollars for that job, I thought of Sherm—perhaps after all he had lived fifty years too early rather than too late as he had expressed it.

Sherm and Blanche liked to sit in the sunshine of the barn door on fine days and watch their neighbors go by, Blanche in a rocking chair with her favorite cat Pansy on her lap. When I think of them, I picture them there. They were the only people I ever knew with such concern for their neighbors that in a night thunderstorm they would get out of bed and dress, ready to help in case lightning struck a house nearby. They were enjoying the color of the autumn trees one day and thought there was more brilliance each passing year—"Maybe it's because we appreciate it more as we grow old," Sherm said.

I miss seeing Sherm hurrying down the road to his shop, thin, bent-shouldered, his large hands and long arms reaching almost to his knees. Could he know the scarcity of good blacksmiths today and how eagerly they are sought by restorers of old houses who need skilled iron-crafters; could he see the increasing number of fine horses exhibited at the fairs which want shoeing as much as horses of an earlier day—he would be happy.

What is more cheerful, now, in the fall of the year, than an open wood-fire? Do you hear those little chirps and twitters coming out of that piece of applewood? Those are the ghosts of the robins and bluebirds that sang upon the bough when it was in blossom last Spring.

—THOMAS BAILEY ALDRICH

NOVEMBER

Birthstone and Birthdays

The Birthstone for November is the *Topaz*, for *Fidelity*.

1	16
2	17
3	18
4	19
5	20
6	21
7	22
8	23
9	24
10	25
11	26
12	27
13	28
14	29
15	30

Flower

THE ROSEMARY
Rosmarinus officinalis

TO EVERY herb lover, Rosemary is for Remembrance. There could be no other meaning for it since the fair Ophelia, in possibly the most moving scene in all of Shakespeare, named the flowers and herbs of her simple bouquet in the madness of her grief.

> There's Rosemary, that's for remembrance; pray you, love,
> remember; and there is pansies, that's for thoughts. . . . There's
> fennel for you, and columbines; there's rue for you, and
> here's some for me; we may call it herb of grace o' Sundays.
> O, you must wear your rue with a difference. There's a
> daisy; I would give you some violets, but they withered all
> when my father died.

Rosemary is one of the most endearing of the herbs. For centuries it has been used in garlands to celebrate weddings and other fêtes. Rosemary was once placed on church altars at Christmas, and is still used in this way occasionally by those who keep old traditions. Branches of Rosemary have been used by New England housewives in linen chests and closets for many generations, to discourage moths and bring a sweet fragrance to the contents. It has always been considered a valuable culinary herb, giving special flavor to fish, salads, lamb, veal, and chicken, but must be used with care, for it is

one of the strong herbs. It also makes a fine tea. The medicinal properties
of Rosemary fill several columns in Nicholas Culpeper's *Herbal* of olden
times. He suggests burning leaves "to correct the air in houses and chambers"
and smoking them like tobacco for curing diseases of the lungs.

At Thanksgiving, a few leaves of Rosemary enhance the flavor of the
turkey gravy. A nosegay of mixed herbs including Rosemary might be tied
with a yellow and brown ribbon and made into a place card for the guests.
An unusual and very effective centerpiece for a Thanksgiving table is a bowl
of fresh herbs—parsley, sage, lemon verbena, and Rosemary, with yellow
chrysanthemums for color.

Rosemary is not winter-hardy in New England, but it flourishes in the
house during the cold months, imparting a fragrance to the room where it
is kept (in a sunny window), and furnishing convenient snippings for cooking. The blue flowers appear in the spring, and I have heard it said that if
the plant is touched lightly by frost in the fall before bringing it into the
house, it will flower in spring more abundantly.

An old adage advises that "The mistress rules the house" where Rosemary flourishes, but we have found it is not necessarily so in our house.

The whole plant has a fragrant and aromatic smell: it is
lighter and more delicate in the flower, and stronger in the leaves.
The taste also is warm and aromatic, and not disagreeable.
The sun claims privilege in it, and it is under the celestial Ram.
It is an herb of as great use with us in these days as any
whatsoever, not only for physical but civil purposes.

—NICHOLAS CULPEPER

Bird

THE WHITE-BREASTED NUTHATCH
Sitta carolinensis

Shrewd little haunter of woods all gray,
Whom I meet on my walk of a winter day
You're busy inspecting each cranny and hole
In the ragged bark of yon hickory bole.

—EDITH M. THOMAS

A COUNTRY name for this eastern bird was "Devil Downhead," from his habit of traveling down and around tree trunks headfirst. There is nothing devilish about the Nuthatch, he is in fact a very friendly and amusing bird who harbors no designs against anything except the insects which riddle our shade and fruit trees, and only then because he must eat them to live.

In November, this neatly attired small bird returns from the woodlands where he spends the summer perhaps but a mile or two away, and inspects all our garden trees from top to bottom, searching tiny crevices in the bark for a good meal of insect eggs, larvae, and hibernating adult bugs and spiders. He is a permanent resident of New England, and like other rugged natives enjoys the change of seasons, the snows and roaring winds, the brilliant sunny days, the exhilaratingly dry, clean, sharp air.

He is one of the winter birds most easily attracted to the bird-feeders, where he finds seeds, grains, oatmeal, and particularly clear beef suet to his special liking. Defying the stormiest of days, he will appear regularly for his dinner, and then disappear heaven knows where to shelter for the night. He is invariably accompanied by his wife, to whom he is happily wedded for life. Like many of his counterparts among the human race, he is extremely kind and solicitous to his wife in the early spring when his fancy turns to thoughts of love, often handing her tidbits. But in winter his attitude is "I'm first served at feeding," and he instructs her in no uncertain bird language to await her turn in a nearby tree while he dines in splendor at the feeder. When he has finished gorging, she will then take her turn at table.

Nuthatches have little fear of anyone who approaches them, but have an amusing way of stretching out their necks while perched upside down under a branch or on a tree trunk, to see what is going on. They are inquisitive, curious little birds, expecting people to be as friendly and harmless as they themselves are.

The Nuthatch wears a sleek full-dress suit of slate-gray with a vest of clean pure white and a black cap, a touch of rusty brown just under the tail. His wife is grayer, but fully as neat as her mate. They have long straight slender bills, which they use to probe the bark for their meals. For their habit of walking upside down around limbs and trunks they are well equipped with long toes, the claws of which are also long, sharp, and thin, enabling them to grip with sure tenacity. If the branches happen to be covered with snow or ice on top, they will simply walk on the bottom of the branch, as easily as a fly on a plastered ceiling. They are said to rest and sleep clinging head down to a branch, but this would be difficult to guarantee.

> I fain would know
> How you can so reckless and fearless go,
> Head upward, head downward, all one to you,
> Zenith and nadir the same in your view.
> —EDITH M. THOMAS

Their most distinguishing mark is the sharp "Hank hank, hank hank" of their call, which is about a B or B-flat on the musical scale. In the early spring, they will sit on a branch and sing a twittering "Sweet sweet sweet sweet" in a musical sort of way, but the song is not notable and is actually seldom heard or identified.

When the Nuthatches disappear from the haunts of people in the nesting season, they retreat into cool deep woods. They nest in cavities. Sometimes they will produce their own nesting holes by pecking into old trees with infinite patience and hard work. But they are quite likely to use old woodpecker or flicker holes, or rotted knotholes. The cavity is first stuffed with small twigs, flakes of bark, grass, and leaves, then lined with fur and feathers. The five to nine eggs are a creamy- or rosy white, lightly speckled with brown and lavender. There are usually two broods. While the female is incubating the eggs, her mate brings food to her and is the soul of domesticity and love.

When these unpretentious, friendly birds come back in pairs to the dooryard in late autumn to begin their light hammering at the trees, they converse with each other in their comical little nasal call-notes, peering inquisitively about them. Soon they will be regular visitors at the feeders and suet boxes, cheerful and amusing and busy the long winter through. The feeders are their salvation during times when ice storms completely encase the branches. Can it be possible that their call then sounds very like "Thanks, thanks"?

Enough Snow to Track a Cat

Over the river and through the wood
Trot fast, my dapple-gray!
Spring over the ground
Like a hunting hound,
For this is Thanksgiving Day.
—LYDIA MARIA CHILD

WASN'T it just yesterday that we were picking daffodils to arrange in a yellow bowl for the summer kitchen table, and in an old lavender teapot for the dining-room mantel? Wasn't it just yesterday that the bluebirds were singing a soft carol from the leafy butternut tree, and the roses were in bloom? Wasn't it just yesterday that the meadowlark called "It's early"? It wasn't yesterday, it was months ago, and now we are planting new daffodils for blossom next spring; the bluebirds are long gone; the butternut tree is bare of leaves and squirrels have cached most of the nuts in the stone wall. Roses are protected for winter. Instead of the song of a meadowlark, we hear the sharp call of the busy nuthatch as he probes the tree trunks for a juicy beetle-steak hidden in cracks of bark. The November wind scurries fitfully and the cold rain falls in a leaden sheet across brown fields.

In the village store and around the firesides, the folklore of winter is discussed, and almanacs are consulted. It's useful to know how much hay cattle will need for their barn feeding, how much wood will have to be brought in, how much protection to give the bees in their snug hives. If winter is to be a hard one, the Butt'ry must have an extra supply of lard and meal and sugar, and an extra barrel of apples will be put into the cellar.

Bees will do their own predicting, if one will heed their signs. If they have laid eggs very late in summer to provide more workers for the hive, the extra workers will be needed, for the winter will be a hard one. If the wax in the combs is thick, on the other hand, the bees do not anticipate a need for all their honey and so they preserve their store of it by a heavy layer of wax.

Young and old in New England know that it is wise to expect a hard winter with plenty of snow if the husks on the corn are unusually thick and difficult to peel off; if the black band around a woolly bear caterpillar is wide; if the peeling on fall apples is tough; if the chipmunks and squirrels steal an unusually large number of butternuts and hazelnuts; if the cattails are very tall and full; if the buds on trees and bushes are covered with a thick and heavy shell; if the hornets have built their nests high in the trees out of danger of snowdrifts.

In our village, predictions on the number of storms to be expected during the coming winter are made by the beloved former schoolteacher "Miz' Prince," who still gathers the village children around her during the school year for her kindergarten. Mrs. Prince has snow-white hair arranged in a neat coiffure, lively blue eyes, and she speaks in a slow precise old-fashioned way that is a delight to hear. "A storm is enough snow to track a cat," she explains. "If you haven't got a cat, why, of course, it's easy enough to step out-of-doors and take a look at your own tracks. To predict the number of storms for the coming winter, you write down the number of the month in which the first storm occurs. Then you add the date of the month on which the storm fell, and then add the number of the day of the week. Then you add the number of days since the last new moon. Now, suppose the first storm fell on Tuesday, November 8; and suppose you look in the almanac and count up to see that there had been 27 days since the last new moon. You would add together the number of 11—for the eleventh month, November—plus 8 for the date of November 8, plus 3 for Tuesday, being the third day of the week, plus 27 for the number of days since the last new moon before that date. This adds up to 49, so I would predict that there would be forty-nine storms during the winter. Last winter I predicted 49 storms and I only missed by a couple—perhaps I counted only one when two storms fell during a twenty-four-hour period. It was a hard winter. I'm usually accurate within a very small margin. Of course, everything is different now that people are going to the moon. I really don't know what's going to become of our old predictions."

We follow her forecasts for winter and prepare for them however forehandedly we can.

On a November day a soft breath of wind from the south may drift into the garden, and we set out chairs on the lawn for an Indian summer reunion with old friends. The sun is warm, the haze over the hills is purple, and there is a balmy fragrance of herbs permeating the air. Nature gives us these few tranquil days of mildness as a special bonus before winter storms set in with their turbulence. We look about us with special appreciation. November woods and fields have a soft beauty of their own. There are no blossoms accenting the fields and woods, but moss glows brightly green in the sunlight and the bare branches of trees and shrubs are outlined in delicate gray tracery against the evergreens. The brown fields and marshes furnish feeding grounds for migrating ducks and songbirds, and a few laggard crows flap across the expanses, their wings silhouetted blackly against the sky.

Along the coasts on a mild November day, the waves break in sullen muffled sound. Flocks of geese head south in perfect V-formation, honking in excited conversation possibly about weather and flying conditions. Lobster pots in the distance bob and dip on the heaving water and gulls cry.

Water in the rain barrel has a thin coat of ice most mornings, which will become thicker with each succeeding day. Finally on an Indian summer day, we turn the barrel over to spill out the water, and leave it upturned for the winter. We put a final dressing of bone meal and compost over all the cleaned garden beds, rake the last blow of leaves, take in the birdbath and the sundial, leaving St. Francis in his niche to watch over the garden for the winter.

November dusk sets in early, and when the wind changes to bring a darkened sky and the first snowflakes of a storm, we hurry in to the Old Kitchen to sort the bayberries we have picked, ready for a late fall evening's candle-dipping.

November was not only Thanksgiving month for our ancestors in America, it was also one of the busiest months of the year. There were the holiday puddings and cakes to be baked, mincemeat to be heaped into a big crock; lye to be made and the soap supply to be prepared. Wood had to be brought into the shed. Hogs were butchered, the meat cured, and hams hung on an iron hook in the fireplace or smokehouse. The last of the harvest was stored. Foundations of house and barn were banked with leaves, sawdust, or pine needles to keep out the cold winds which crept through the underpinnings. Threads and yarns must be spun, and dyes prepared for use all winter in supplying the family with hand-woven cloth for wearing and household use. Each evening as the family gathered around the warm hearth to complete the tasks of the household, the hum of the spinning wheel and the soft pounding of the loom batten were heard.

Candles must be dipped in November, too. Some candles were made of beef and mutton tallow, and they smoked and smelled when burned. Bayberry candles perfumed the air and burned without smoking.

Directions for making bayberry candles say, "Boil the berries in a kettle of water, let cool, skim off the layer of wax the berries leave. Melt this wax in a kettle and dip wicking until well coated." Few of the directions tell how many bushels of bayberries it would take to produce enough candles for a winter's use; but I have used something like a half-bushel of berries to produce a single candle. Nevertheless, bayberry candles have been made in New England for centuries now. It is traditional that for good fortune they are burned constantly until they are gone. One old book explained, however, that "If accident puts a candle out, it yields a pleasant fragrancy to all that are in the room; insomuch that nice people often put them out on purpose to have the incense of the expiring stuff." Considering the amount of bayberries needed and the tediousness of making bayberry candles, it is a wonder they were ever burned at all except for holidays or emergencies, but they burn slowly and steadily with a bright flame, so in a way they are economical if plenty of berries are available. A pair of hand-dipped bayberry candles tied with a gay red bow and a sprig of pine is one of the most luxurious Christmas presents one can give.

Christmas!—we count the days now and begin preparations for making presents and stocking up the Butt'ry for the holiday season. We wind a warp for the old loom, and sley the reed with linen for placemats and napkins, or with handspun wool for scarves, or with gay cotton for hand towels, presents which must be finished to put under the Christmas tree.

The old loom stood in the loft of a barn when we found it, its heddle frames on the floor nearly buried in the chaff of a century or more of disuse, its beams entwined in dusty cobwebs. It has recovered its pride and its usefulness in our weaving shed, and on a quiet day there is deep satisfaction and pleasure in producing a length of cloth with rhythmic beat and count. The art and skill of weaving is being revived after many years of oblivion which followed the invention of spinning and weaving machinery. Fortunately, prized heirloom pieces of hand weaving were kept, and at least one of the great American hand weavers, "Weaver Rose" of Kingston, Rhode Island, kept detailed notes on many of his best patterns so that we can reproduce them today with little difficulty.

November is the month to think about winter's provision for the birds. We take stock of the trees and shrubs we have planted or saved for their delectation and count a dozen or so which are laden with bright fruit in

season—dogwood, shadbush, blueberry, chokecherry, mulberry, high-bush cran-
berry, euonymus, mountain ash, hawthorn and apple, birches (birds love the
tiny seeds in winter), bayberry, inkberry, and the native New England holly,
black alder (*Ilex verticillata*).

For their protection and nesting we let vines grow in summer over the
arbors, fences, and stone walls, and high into dead trees down the lane and
along the edges of woods: honeysuckle, woodbine, bittersweet, wild grapes,
turquoise berry, and wild clematis.

While songbirds have been one of man's best friends in protecting crops
from insects, providing food when necessary, in giving delightful company
to many whose lives are lonely or colorless, man in turn is the birds' worst
enemy, with his guns, sprays, and poisons, and his destruction of the birds'
natural habitats and food supplies employed in the name of progress. Song-
bird enemies next in importance are cats, who cannot help their hunting
instincts; English sparrows and starlings who usurp nesting and feeding sites.
Until Europeans came to take over this land, birds maintained an ecological
balance of their own with their natural enemies. But they have not been able
to hold their own with the men, cats, starlings, and sparrows now living
here who are not indigenous to the country.

To compensate for this imbalance, the feeding of birds and extra provision for nesting accommodations has become necessary to prevent their
extermination. The results of such programs are showing. Bluebirds seem to
be coming back (although the passenger pigeon never will); orioles once
more sing from our trees; large flocks of birds are saved from starvation in
winter by feeding programs carried on by householders everywhere. Birds
which previously seldom strayed into New England because of lack of winter
food are now staying all winter long, well fed, sheltered, and happy.

Since songbirds can live scarcely longer than twenty-four hours without
food, it is wise to keep the feeders well stocked from the first snowstorm
until spring brings them a supply of their natural food. Early November is

the time to start a regime of daily filling of bird-feeders. In the spring, the feeding is gradually tapered off and it is not wise to feed birds during the summer months. If they and their young of the year learn to depend upon feeding in summer, they will be unable to fend for themselves when the need arises.

Feeders ought to be sheltered from prevailing winds and storms. If squirrels and unwelcome birds come to the feeder, they can often be enticed to a different area by a supply of cracked corn at some distance from the small bird-feeders.

With a thrift suitable to the New England household, we save for the birds—seeds from the garden and fields of sunflowers, sumac, and thistles. We save clear white beef suet, and sometimes make a Thanksgiving pudding of melted suet or unsalted fat mixed with small seeds, cracked corn, apple and sunflower and squash and pumpkin seeds. Bread and cooky and graham cracker crumbs are saved; doughnuts and cake which have become stale; apple cores and raisins, leftover cooked oatmeal. We save pine, fir, and spruce cones and dip them in unsalted fat to hang outside the window or in nearby trees. We save bits of sandwiches or lettuce left on a luncheon plate, and hang old ears of dried corn for bluejays and squirrels. We save scraps of crumbled dogfood, cooked fish, and hard-boiled eggs, even the eggshells.

It is a maxim that nothing goes to waste in a New England household. In colorful cross-stitch, the motto "Waste Not, Want Not" hangs on many a kitchen wall. Not even a bone is willfully thrown away until every bit of good has been squeezed out of it. Rib roast of beef bones make the best of soups. Ham bones give rich flavor to split pea soup. Turkey bones left from Thanksgiving dinner make Turkey Soup with Rice or Curried Turkey Soup which we relish nearly as much as the roasted bird. Steak bones are saved to make stock for Ginette's French Onion Soup which we learned to make in France, as we mentioned in September. And what is so good as soup on a blustery November night? We serve it in our best Staffordshire tureen and light candles on table and mantel.

RICH BEEF SOUP

Remove excess fat from "remainder bones" of a cooked rib roast of beef, leaving on as much meat as possible. In a large kettle, put bones and enough water to cover; 1 tsp. of salt per quart of water, 1 peeled sliced onion, a Tbs. of mixed herbs, chopped celery, or lovage leaves, a sliced carrot, 6 or 8 peppercorns, and 4 whole cloves. Simmer gently, adding a little water if necessary to keep bones covered, until meat comes off bones easily with a fork. Reserve meat (discard bones or give to the dog for an afternoon snack), strain the soup.

Return the soup with the addition of the meat to the fire; add 1 fresh sliced carrot, a small diced onion, several tomatoes peeled and quartered. Simmer until carrot is tender (25–30 minutes). Add 1 Tbs. chopped parsley. Taste for seasoning, adding more salt or pepper if needed. One's ingenuity will produce other additions to benefit the soup—a dollop of red wine or a teaspoon of Worcestershire sauce, a bit of turnip, a few peas or beans, left-over beef gravy.

Serve from a tureen, being sure to put some of the meat and vegetables into each bowlful. It is permissible to break crackers into this soup at our house.

SPLIT PEA SOUP

In a large kettle put 2½ to 3 quarts of water and bring to a boil. Add the bone from a ham, 1 small diced onion, and 1 lb. green split dried peas. Cook at a simmer for about 2½ hours or until peas are very soft. Stir occasionally to keep peas from sticking to bottom of kettle.

Remove from fire and let cool. Remove ham bone, dice the meat which can be cut easily from the bones, and return meat to the kettle, discarding bone. Add more water if soup is too thick. Heat to simmer, taste for seasoning. Add 1 tsp. fresh chopped (or ½ tsp. dried) basil leaves to the pot; or add a small pinch of the leaves to each bowlful. Some people like the soup put through a food mill, but we prefer ours with the peas and ham bits left for texture and appearance. Serve piping hot, with a teaspoon of sour cream or herb butter on the top.

TURKEY SOUP

Into a large kettle put the remainder bones of a cooked turkey. Add water to cover generously; add 1 sliced onion, a Tbs. of fresh or dried herbs, several celery or lovage leaves, salt and pepper. If there is leftover turkey gravy, this may be added, too. Simmer gently for about 3 hours until meat comes off bones easily; remove from heat and let it cool.

When cool, remove most of the layer of fat from the top. Remove turkey bones and pick off all the bits of meat and return meat to the soup stock. Discard bones (*don't* give them to the dog). Add ½ cup of rice, salt and pepper if needed. Bring to a simmer and cook 20 minutes or until rice is tender. Serve from a tureen with plenty of turkey bits for each serving.

To make Curried Turkey Soup, proceed as above, except, in place of rice, mix ½ cup of flour and enough water to dissolve flour in a screw-top jar, shake well until smooth and add to the soup. Stir in well and simmer for 20 minutes. Add curry powder to taste with the last simmering.

GINETTE'S FRENCH ONION SOUP

Prepare beef consommé by simmering the bones from a large sirloin steak for several hours in 4 cups of water. Let it simmer down to 2 cups of consommé. Strain.

Peel, then slice very thinly, 1½ lbs. white onions; in a large frying pan melt 2 Tbs. butter, add the sliced onions, and cook at medium heat until onions are a nice golden brown, about 10 minutes. Add 2 Tbs. flour and stir in well. Pour in 4 cups boiling water and 2 cups of the hot beef consommé. Cover lightly and simmer slowly for 10 minutes, add salt and pepper to taste.

While the soup is cooking, dry in the oven, or toast, as many thin slices of French bread as will cover the bottom of a deep ovenproof casserole or *cocotte*. Or put one slice in the bottom of each of several individual *petites marmites* of ovenproof pottery. Remove soup pan from fire; add a generous tablespoon of thick cream. Empty the soup into the *cocotte* (or *petites marmites*), not too full. The bread comes to the top. Cover bread with 3 or 4 Tbs. of grated Gruyère or Swiss cheese, and put the dish in the oven at medium heat, 350° for about 20 minutes. Serve in the dish, very hot. *Bon appétit.*

The Mock Turtle sighed deeply, and began, in a voice choked with sobs, to sing this:—"Beautiful Soup, so rich and green, Waiting in a hot tureen! Who for such dainties would not stoop? Soup of the evening, beautiful Soup! Soup of the evening, beautiful Soup!"

—LEWIS CARROLL, *Alice's Adventures in Wonderland*

Portrait—Weaver Rose

AN ARTIST IN YARNS

HE WAS perhaps a hundred years behind the times, wore a long white beard, and went barefoot. But he was the darling of the fashionable Narragansett Bay society ladies in Rhode Island all of his adult life. His name was William Henry Harrison Rose, although he was known to many as "Quaker Billy" or just "Weaver" Rose.

The secret of his success was not his social presence, for he had none. He was a shy, diffident man who shunned people when he could; but since his livelihood depended on people, he was courteous enough, receiving visitors with a very few kindly words, and even perhaps an offer of snuff which he took constantly.

Weaver Rose was born and lived all his life in a rambling weather-beaten farm cottage near Kingston, Rhode Island, surrounded by great trees, stone walls, fields, and flowers. He never married. His spinster sister Elsie kept house for him. Both were considered in the neighborhood to be eccentric.

Someone we know remembers that as a child he visited the Rose farm with his father, seeking out the man whom all of South County found it so intriguing and worthwhile to know. At the time of this visit, Weaver Rose's sister explained that Billy was in the field hoeing his garden but that she would call him. She picked up a conch shell, lifted it to her lips and blew into it a long clear blast, which indeed brought Billy in from the field.

He was barefoot as usual, and clad in overalls and a plain natural-color woolen shirt. His clean long white hair and beard hung in soft waves over his shoulders and chest, his blue eyes twinkled in greeting, and he invited the man and boy into his cottage, which was filled with many beautiful and fascinating things.

No, the secret of his success was not his social presence. It was his skill as a hand weaver which made him so popular. His father had been a farmer, but Weaver Rose had learned from his grandparents the gentle craft of weaving yarns and threads into beautiful fabrics. He wove coverlets, rugs, pillowcovers, draperies. It is said that one of his rich customers left him a piece of ribbon from her garter as a guide to the color she wanted in a couch cover. He was best known for the coverlets and "hap-harlots" (a medieval term for a coarse woolen bedcover) which he wove in quantity. Most of these coverlets were in the popular old-fashioned colors of blue and white and they were woven in old-fashioned patterns with names like "Church Steps," "Rail Fence," "Orange Peel," and "Pansies in the Wilderness."

To the weavers of today, the name of Weaver Rose is a familiar one although few have ever seen him (he died in 1913 and his picturesque cottage burned to the ground about 1930). For Weaver Rose kept alive the craft of hand weaving at a time when others had forsaken it due to the rapid rise in the easy and cheap power-spinning and weaving techniques. His skill was unsurpassed, and he worked from a worn pattern book which contained over one hundred of the old overshot patterns handed down from the many generations of American weavers who preceded him. It is not known definitely whether these patterns were original with Weaver Rose but he was known to exchange patterns generously with others interested in weaving techniques. These patterns which he so carefully saved are once again being used by hand weavers across the country, and to Weaver Rose is given the credit for nurturing and even reviving a craft which might otherwise have been lost to the present and future generations of weavers.

Weaver Rose had many looms, all made by hand, as well as other equipment necessary to his trade such as winders, shuttles, warping devices, raddles, and spinning wheels. He was known to say that he could make more money at weaving than he could by farming. "I have wove 30 yards of carpet in one day at 10 cents a yard," he once wrote a friend. And he felt that he was well-enough paid.

As a rule the weaver asked for payment for his goods on delivery. But there must have come a time when some of the payments faltered, for among his possessions was found a poem which he composed:

> Come ye Patrones Proud and Lowley
> Rich and Raged, Every Man
> Come and Fork over what you owe
> The Poor old weaver Man.
> We are rite Anxious to Receve it
> Oh, we Sadley Nead the Chink,
> Every Dollar Bright Believe It
> To Pay for Weaving Warp and Wullen.
> Pray Dont hesitate ye byers
> Of the Weavers Pittance Think
> Send o Send the Silver Shiners
> Quickly Cash us or We Sink.

Weavers of today are grateful that Weaver Rose's artistry in yarns exceeded greatly his skill at verse.

One of the old looms which belonged to Weaver Rose, and to his grandfather before him, is now housed in the restored old Watson House on the campus of the University of Rhode Island at Kingston (open daily to the public), only a few miles from the corner of three townships where it stood so long in the ell of the Rose cottage. It has a warp stretched across its wide beam, and occasionally an interested craftsman in the Home Economics Department of the University takes a few throws with a shuttle. Its use there is more sentimental than practical, which might sadden Quaker Billy, who was proud of being a useful craftsman, the last of the old-time Rhode Island hand weavers.

A Prayer of Thanksgiving

We praise Thee, O God, for the order and constancy of nature;
for the beauty and bounty of the world; for day and night,
summer and winter, seedtime and harvest; for the varied gifts of
loveliness and use which every season brings.

DECEMBER

Birthstone and Birthdays

The Birthstone for December is the *Turquoise,* or the *Lapis Lazuli,* for *Prosperity.*

1		16
2		17
3		18
4		19
5		20
6		21
7		22
8		23
9		24
10		25
11		26
12		27
13		28
14		29
15		30
		31

Flower

THE BOXWOOD
Buxus sempervirens

ALTHOUGH there are several varieties of Boxwood, the Common Box is the most familiar one, as its name suggests. It has been planted in New England since early colonial gardens were laid out. A dark evergreen shrub with inconspicuous flowers, it grows along the New England coastal areas in gardens, and also inland where some winter protection from drying winds and sun can be provided, like any hardy broad-leaved evergreen. It is slow-growing, but lends itself to pruning and trimming. Most of the topiary work found in formal gardens is Boxwood. Sometimes the wood, which is hard and smooth, is used for making fine musical instruments, for fine carving and engraving.

The Boxwood has a pungent fragrance which is unmistakable once identified, and on a humid day just a hint of this fragrance will bring to mind walks in old English lanes, or chateau gardens of France, or old-fashioned gardens in Williamsburg, Mount Vernon, Charlottesville, or in Old Essex, Stonington, Wickford, Beacon Hill, or Salem.

Boxwood is easily propagated by four- or five-inch stem cuttings taken in the fall and rooted in damp sand or vermiculite. In the dwarf form the shrub makes an easily controlled and delightful edging for herb gardens and flower beds. In the regular form, the bushes make softly rounded outlines and accents in the garden, restful in their dark-green color and pleasant in their fragrance.

The sentimental meaning of Box is "Constancy." Sarah Josepha Hale wrote a poem in this vein for her volume *Flora's Interpreter*:

> Though youth be past, and beauty fled,
> The constant heart its pledge redeems
> Like Box, that guards the flowering bed,
> And brighter from the contrast seems.

At Christmas, Boxwood cuttings are used for wreaths, kissing balls, topiary Christmas trees for tables and hallways, swags and ropes, and gay decorations for doors and windows.

> Holly and Ivy, Box and Bay
> Put in the church on Christmas Day.
> —A fifteenth-century
> Christmas carol

Bird

THE CARDINAL
Richmondea cardinalis

IT'S A HABIT in New England to look back on "the good old days" when (we like to think) life was more interesting, more gracious and more colorful. That this isn't completely true is evidenced by the gaiety with which we now celebrate Christmas contrasted with the grim days of Puritanism when Christmas festivities were banned. And in the good old days, New England was visited by many families who came only to spend their summer holidays, leaving the cold snow-clad hills and long smooth white valleys of winter to the natives. Nowadays, in addition to the summer vacationers, in winter too the hills and valleys are filled with colorful visitors. They come to ski or tobogan or snowmobile or just to look. And from all parts of the country, people who have come to visit have very often found New England so beautiful, so congenial, so stimulating that they stay and make their homes here.

There is a bird counterpart of the change that has come over New England in these respects. That bird is the Cardinal, also called the Redbird. This handsome, aristocratic, grand opera star from the southland has come to New England sometime in the last few decades to look around and to pay us perhaps a brief call. Like other musicians and gifted folk, he liked what he found and so has stayed in some sections of New England to be a year-round resident whose flashing red coat makes a great splash of color in nature's northeast winter landscape. In addition, he is the very symbol of the warmth and joy with which all New Englanders now celebrate Christmas.

Perfectly in season for Christmas are his coat of brilliant red and his wife's gown of greenish tinge. His loud, clear call of "Cheer, cheer, *what* cheer *what* cheer *what* cheer!" gives us the best possible Christmas greeting.

Cardinals are native southern birds which do not migrate but do occasionally wander a bit, which is how they got into New England. Their presence is so welcome that wherever they have been seen, bird lovers have laid a sumptuous banquet table to entice them to stay. They have found New England's woodland borders, brushy banks of streams, thicketed valleys, wooded parks, and gardens sheltered from the coldest winds to be of special congeniality, and they may now be found here across much of New England all year round.

The male Cardinal is unmistakable with his vermilion red suit and his regal crest, his carnival mask of black and his thick red bill. His wife's gown is quieter in color with greenish-brown on her back and soft splashes of red. She often joins her mate in singing a duet of arresting musical notes. They are the finest of opera singers, with rich powerful voices thrilling to hear. They like the center of the stage when performing, usually the topmost branch of a tree. There are several songs in the repertoire which they repeat as it suits them. It is impossible not to stop and listen when this concert is in progress.

Cardinals sing freely in spring and summer but after mating and during nesting they tend to be rather quiet and secretive, not wanting to call attention to the young in the nest. However, if they have adopted for a building site a vine clinging to the porch pillar or a bush in the dooryard, their flashing color is such that their activities cannot be kept secret and the progress of nesting can be watched.

Their nest is built rather near the ground in bushy woodland thickets or tangles of vines, sometimes in a pyracantha or holly bush. The nest is loosely constructed of twigs and stems, leaves and fibers lined with grasses and hair. Three or four white or greenish-white eggs spotted with reddish-brown are laid, and in New England two broods are usual; in the longer season of more southerly states there will often be three broods. Their habit of building the nest near the ground makes the baby birds particularly inviting and convenient to the depredations of cats, and the parent birds do not have an easy time in successfully raising their families. Another of their predilections is an extreme jealousy which sometimes causes them to battle their own reflections in windows. They will fly with rage at the images with such force that their necks or wings may be broken.

The male Cardinal is a good husband and a proud parent, a fond family bird. He feeds the mother bird while she is on the nest and takes on the job of feeding the fledglings when they leave the nest, while the mother goes about her housework of the second brooding.

In winter amid the falling snowflakes these graceful, richly garbed, and full-voiced birds with their lordly look are the most welcome and certainly the handsomest of birds at the bird-feeder. There they insist on having their aristocratic rights respected. The male eats first while the female perches on a nearby tree. Then she eats. After that they are quite gracious in allowing other birds to join them at lunch. They search the fields and gardens for dried weed seeds, frozen grapes which may be still clinging to the vines, and for bird-feeders. Their favorite food without any doubt is sunflower, melon, pumpkin, and squash seeds, and cracked corn. Anyone who keeps a good supply of these in the feeders for them will be repaid in pleasure many times just by their presence.

This visitor who has turned New England resident can bring a great thrill when his scarlet coat flashes through a blossoming lilac bush or dogwood tree in spring. But the prettiest Christmas picture imaginable is to see him with his friends, birds of the same feather, perching on a garden fence in the snow. He does not sing operatic arias in winter but he frequently calls in a clear whistle which anticipates for us the coming concerts of spring and summer.

No Heaven can come to us unless our hearts find rest in
today. Take Heaven!

No peace lies in the future which is not hidden in this present
instant. Take Peace!

The gloom of the world is but a shadow. Behind it, yet within
reach . . . is Joy.

There is a radiance and glory in the darkness, could we but see,
and to see we have only to look; I beseech you to
look.

—FRA GIOVANNI DI CAPISTRANO

Seven Dozen Wax Tapers

Announced by all the trumpets of the sky,
Arrives the snow, and, driving o'er the fields,
Seems nowhere to alight: the whited air
Hides hills and woods, the river, and the heaven,
And veils the farm-house at the garden's end.
—RALPH WALDO EMERSON

THE noonday sun, low in the southern winter sky, bathes the Old Kitchen with a warm light. There is an air of happy busyness about the house for presents are being wrapped, cards are handwritten with special messages for old friends, cookies are baked and packed into gay boxes and jars, wreaths are fashioned, friends greeted.

Out-of-doors the days can be crystal clear; or they can be sullen and gray with sleet pelting the windows. Snow must be dusted off the Yule log and a bow of red with a sprig of rosemary tied about its middle readied for the ceremony of carrying it in from the woodshed and burning it at the proper time. Sleigh bells, which used to ring with gay rhythm from the harnesses of Grandfather's prancing horses, now are hung upon the doors to announce the coming of visitors. In our old house, as in all of New England, as in all of America, Christmas preparations are being made for the celebration of the Nativity in church and home. It was not always so in New England.

During the Middle Ages in Europe, the church was in its greatest splendor and Christmas celebrations were extremely beautiful. But in time the festival degenerated into a secular season of boisterous mischief, drinking, and gambling which was so distasteful and so bitterly opposed by the Protestants led by Oliver Cromwell that when they came to power in England they abolished the observance of Christmas in church, home, and country. Henceforth it was considered a day of work. According to their reasoning, a celebration in observance of Christ's birthday had not been ordained in the Bible; therefore it must not be included in their religious observances. Strong punishments were meted out to those who disobeyed the law.

On Christmas Day 1620, the Puritans, who had just landed on the shores of their new land, worked at the construction of their first building in purposeful neglect of the day. The following year, in 1621, Governor Bradford publicly reprimanded several "lustye younge men" who declined to work on Christmas Day.

Since there were apparently those who still managed to observe Christmas in some way, in 1659 the Puritans enacted a law in Massachusetts to punish anyone who kept Christmas, and a fine of five shillings was designated for each offense. And so for a long time, Christmas came to be virtually ignored in New England by those of the Puritan faith as well as Presbyterians, Baptists, and Quakers who found their way to the area.

It is also true that not every man who came to America was persuaded that Christmas was not a time for joy. John Alden, for example, came with the Puritans as a paid worker (he was a cooper) and not necessarily to seek religious freedom. Soon members of the Church of England, the Episcopalians, were established along the New England seacoast in such areas as Rhode Island, and Portsmouth, New Hampshire. Eventually there were Catholics and Lutherans established in the new country, and there were probably a good many of no particular religious beliefs to whom Christmas nevertheless was remembered as a time of joy. And joy cannot long be repressed.

By 1681 the strict law against the celebrating of Christmas was repealed in Massachusetts, probably because it became difficult to enforce. For members of the Episcopal churches, the communion and observance of Christmas was one of their most important religious days. They held services wherever they could, enjoying as best they could the festival season with worship, with visiting and feasting. By 1686 there was actually a Christmas service held at the Town Hall in Boston.

Thanksgiving was the most important and most generally celebrated day of feasting and merrymaking, but in many homes and churches there were those who celebrated Christmas quietly in a proper observance of the true spirit of the day. As in times of old, in the taverns men who gathered for the discussion of political affairs would sometimes lift a cup to wish their neighbors and friends a Merry Christmas.

Gradually there was a lessening of opposition to the observance of Christmas. The Puritans themselves, however, continued to ignore Christmas during all of the seventeenth and eighteenth centuries, and in some places this was true well into the nineteenth century. During the American Revolution, General Washington surprised and defeated the Hessian troops when he crossed the Delaware during their Christmas revels, and one can almost see the nodding Puritan heads at the New England taverns approving General Washington's strategy in taking advantage of those who would celebrate on this day.

Far back in the snow-covered hills of New Hampshire, Enoch Little II and his wife Polly moved into their new house as bride and bridegroom in December 1791. In their diaries they failed to mention Christmas in any way until 1823, when they entered this notation: "Meetinghouse finished, shed ground sold, pews sold and Bell hung and House [meeting house] Dedicated on Christmas Day. Good weather—a full house." On December 25, 1827, however, there were no such observances, for "Christmas pleasant; went to mill—6 bushels wheat and one of Indian [corn]." Nearly fifty years later, one of their descendants noted on December 25, 1874: "Cold—Christmas Festival in the evening."

On December 29, 1815, the Newburyport *Herald* in Massachusetts published a controversy between two gentlemen who were called by the newspaper "The Inquirer" and "Philo," in which the celebrating of Christmas was discussed quite candidly in print for perhaps the first time. "The real question is whether the observance of Christmas is a matter of divine appointment," asserted The Inquirer. And he reiterated the Puritan belief that "Thou shalt not add nor diminish" what the Bible ordained and it had *not* ordained a celebration of the birth of Christ.

Philo answered, "But in Luke II, verses 6 to 15 is described the celebration of a multitude of angels, a heavenly host praising God and saying, 'Glory to God in the highest, and on earth peace, good will toward men,' apparently for the purpose of exhibiting a suitable precedent for the Christian World. This should be sufficient to satisfy the most skeptical and cavilling mind."

The entering wedge had been made for New Englanders. By this time Congress in Washington and many state legislatures were adjourning their sessions over the Christmas period, choosing not to profane the holy time with secular concerns.

The first Christmas concert to be held in Boston was given in 1815 by the Handel and Haydn Society at Old King's Chapel, and gradually music became accepted as a fitting observance of the day. In New York in December 1823, Clement Moore wrote a poem called "A Visit from St. Nicholas" whose lines beginning " 'Twas the night before Christmas . . ." swept the country.

At Harvard University, a young German, Charles Follen, arrived to teach, bringing with him from his native land the custom of putting up a Christmas tree. This he did for his young son and decorated it gaily. The first such tree at his home was in 1832, when handmade ornaments, toys, and "seven dozen wax tapers" were affixed to the tree, and neighbors came to see it. How could those stern New England neighbors have glimpsed the warmth and excitement of the day and not been moved to wish it for their own families?

The first White House Christmas tree was introduced during President Pierce's term—and he a New Englander. In England, Charles Dickens was writing stories of Christmas which became very popular and widely read in America, and Tiny Tim and Scrooge became household words depicting the need for thinking of those less fortunate at Christmas time. In Boston finally, lighted candles were being placed in windows on Christmas Eve, bell ringers appeared and carols were sung. This custom on Beacon Hill persists to this day, so that people drive for many miles to see the stately, garlanded doorways, the soft lights in the many-paned windows, and to hear the music of old Boston's traditional Christmas observance.

On December 24, 1853, the South Parish Sunday School in Portsmouth, New Hampshire, had celebrated a Christmas Eve for the children with an elaborate program consisting of storytelling, carol-singing, and a sermon. All over New England many Sunday Schools were decorating the churches for the children, putting up trees and having Christmas celebrations which had long been suppressed.

A delightful old book describing the life of a young girl in Salem, Massachusetts, around 1860 tells of Christmas in that bedrock Puritan town. "The season was celebrated with decorous merriment in our homes," said the author, "but almost no church adornment was seen and most of the shops relaxed not from their customary Salem air of eminent and grave respectability. No butcher sent home a spray of holly with the goose, and no Christmas cards were dropped from the packages of baker or candlestick maker. But in the little shop around the Essex Street corner the very heart and soul of Christmastide dwelt in the plump body of the red-cheeked man who kept that shop. This tiny shop was overflowing with the subtle and joyous spirit of keeping holiday."

Christmas was finally established as a legal holiday in all the New England states: Connecticut in 1845, Vermont in 1850, Rhode Island in 1852, Massachusetts in 1855, Maine in 1858, and New Hampshire in 1861.

In 1875 Louis Prang of Boston put the first American Christmas card on the market, doubtful of its success, yet hopeful. It was popular immediately. Among Mr. Prang's lithographed designs were colorful pictures of the Nativity, of Santa Claus, of children and pretty young women, flowers, birds and butterflies, holly and ivy. The verses were short and simple. Mr. Currier and Mr. Ives printed and sold lithographs of children bringing in the Christmas tree, of great country inns with windows gleaming with light and sleighs filled with fur-clad merrymakers, which were popular best-sellers.

Celebrations in even the most austere Puritan homes began taking on special characteristics from the many people of foreign birth who came to these shores, which gave the Christmas season a genuine American democratic flavor.

From the Germans came the tree with its decorations of cookies, apples, strings of popcorn and sugar candies, paper cornucopias, and "seven dozen wax tapers." From them, too, came blown-glass ornaments shaped like birds, tiny houses and churches, musical instruments, bells, fruits, and angels, some of which may still be found in our attics and antique shops. From the Dutch came St. Nicholas who became our Santa Claus, to bring toys for the children who had been good and sour lemons or switches for those who had been bad. (Where is there a bad child at Christmas?) From the Scandinavian countries came the Advent Wreath and the Advent Calendars. From Italy, the south of France, and Spain came the crêche with all its figures depicting the Nativity, the custom having originated in 1223 when St. Francis of Assisi set up a human pantomime to teach the story of the birth of Christ to the illiterate peasants who gathered around him.

From the British Isles came the custom of the Yule log; of decorating churches and homes with holly, mistletoe, wreaths of rosemary and box and yew; of feasting with plum puddings and mince pies. From the English, too, came the custom of visiting in good fellowship with neighbors and friends, of singing madrigals and carols, of shouting "Merry Christmas," which in very early days meant a blessed or a peaceful Christmas. In ancient Britain, hand-blown colored glass balls were suspended from cords hung on the ceilings and windows. They were called "Witches Balls" and were meant to scare away the evil spirits. It is thought that our round, colored-glass tree ornaments came from this superstitious tradition.

In a New England *Almanac* for December 1704, appeared this verse:

> The days are short, the weather's cold,
> By tavern fires tales are told.
> Some ask for dram when first come in,
> Others with flip and bounce begin.

The old taverns were inviting gathering places for the menfolk of early America, warming themselves by the great hearths, by the heat of discussion, and by the fires of well-spiked beverages. On the shelves of the bars within the tavern corner were an array of bottles of New England rum, wines, cider, and beer; pewter mugs, handsomely blown, and etched flip and wineglasses, jars of spices. Along the coastal areas, taverns were well provided with fresh fruits such as lemons, limes, oranges, and pineapples brought in great sailing ships from romantic tropical countries.

Tavern hosts were citizens of repute and responsibility and they mixed and dispensed the drinks themselves. For special occasions gentlemen often gathered in groups, and sometimes for balls and parties their ladies were included. At such gay times the taverns' best ingredients were mixed with care to produce fine beverages. At Christmas, depending on local beliefs and customs, the old English tradition of the wassail bowl was occasionally revived; or a bowl of punch was passed around; or as the verse above suggests, varied other drinks were consumed.

The equipage for the wassailing consisted of the bowl, the ladle, the nutmeg grater, and the mugs or glasses. In the best taverns and the richest homes, this equipment was often elaborate. Punch bowls were known in New England from 1682 when John Winthrop wrote of the sale of such a bowl in Boston. Dinners were prefaced by drinking punch, sometimes out of the bowl itself as it was passed from hand to hand. These bowls and their ladles were of pewter or of finely made silver, sometimes of porcelain. Thin hand-blown glasses, or mugs of silver or pewter, or even of wood, were used. Since nutmeg was dusted atop most colonial drinks, silver graters in the form of tiny boxes with hinged or screw tops were carried by fine gentlemen in their waistcoat pockets. These skillfully made little boxes housed the nutmeg and provided a miniature pierced grater, and the aromatic spice flavored both food and drink.

The original meaning of the word "Wassail" remains rather obscure, but it may have meant "Be Thou Well," or a kind of "Here's-to-you" toast of good will not necessarily confined to Christmas festivities. The early custom was for a servant or the host to bring in a bowl filled with appropriate liquor made from cider, ale, wine or rum and spices, usually heated and with roasted apples bobbing about on top. As he did so, he would call "Wassail! wassail! wassail!" The merrymakers gathered about the great room of the tavern would fill their mugs or glasses from the bowl and then lift them in a toast, saying "All hail!" This ceremony has carried over in our custom of sharing the Christmas season with friends and neighbors with a bowl of spiced punch or eggnog or syllabub, not always with such picturesque drama perhaps.

In old American receipt books, some interesting concoctions are found for such drinks. Our favorite rule for making a suitable Wassail cup enlivens the serious pages of America's first cookbook. This little book of forty-eight pages called *American Cookery* was published in Hartford, Connecticut, in 1796 and was written by an orphan, Miss Amelia Simmons. Two original copies of the book are in public collections, one in the New York Public Library (the Whitney Collection) and the other in the Library of Congress (the Bitting Collection); and copies are owned by several private collectors.

Miss Simmons gives suggestions (among other interesting things) on how to "Choofe a Peacock for Roafting"; "How to Smother a Fowl in Oyfters"; and—best of all—"To Make a Fine Syllabub from the Cow." This receipt is easy if one has the proper equipment:

TO MAKE A FINE SYLLABUB FROM THE COW

"Sweeten a quart of cyder with double refined sugar, grate nutmeg into it, then milk your cow into your liquor, when you have thus added what quantity of milk you think propcr, pour half a pint or more, in proportion to the quantity of syllabub you make, of the sweeteft cream you can get all over it."

Sack Posset was a kind of sherry eggnog and was a very popular drink in New England for special occasions, including, eventually, Christmas. *Mackenzie's Five Thousand Receipts* was probably the first do-it-yourself book for both husband and wife, published in this country in 1829. Among its five thousand receipts are many for making wine, beer, liqueurs of various kinds, and for popular drinks including

SACK POSSET

"Beat up the yolks and whites of 15 eggs, strain them, and then put three quarters of a pound of white sugar in a pint of Canary [-wine, 'sack' or sherry], and mix it with the eggs in a basin. Set it over a chafing dish of coals, and keep continually stirring it until it is quite hot. Next grate some nutmeg in a quart of milk, boil it, and then pour it into the eggs and wine; while pouring, hold the hand very high, and let another person keep stirring the posset, which renders it smooth, and full bodied to the taste."

AMERICAN FLIP

In Alice Morse Earle's *Stagecoach and Tavern Days* she gives directions for making American Flip. It was made in a great pewter mug or earthen pitcher filled two-thirds full of strong beer; sweetened with sugar, molasses, or diced pumpkin, and flavored with a "dash"—about a half-cup—of New England rum. Into this was thrust and stirred a red-hot loggerhead made of iron and shaped like a poker. The seething iron made the liquor foam and bubble high, giving it a burnt, bitter taste.

Since the Puritans probably came to accept the celebrating of Christmas for the sake of their children, and since children's Christmas parties are as always even more important than those for the grown-ups, we turned to *An Apple a Day*, an old-fashioned dictionary of apple cookery compiled by Leah Inman Lapham, to find her suggestion for a Christmas punch for children which might have been used a hundred years ago. We found an appropriate receipt which has the added qualities of being good for children and grown-ups with twentieth-century tastes.

CHRISTMAS WASSAIL

Combine 1 quart apple cider, 1 cup water, ½ cup brown sugar, ½ lemon sliced thin, ½ orange sliced thin, 1 stick cinnamon, and ¼ tsp. nutmeg. Heat to boiling. Simmer 10 minutes. Strain. Serve hot in bowl or in mugs garnished with a sprig of mint or lemon slice. May also be served cold. Makes 8 servings and is easily enlarged for more people.

"We Wish You a Merry Christmas" with an old family receipt for Figgy Pudding and its sauce. It is best served with an accompaniment of cheerful voices singing the folksong which brought it fame.

FIGGY PUDDING

Stir together 2 beaten eggs and 1 cup sugar. Add and stir into the egg mixture:

1 cup ground or finely chopped	1 cup milk
dried figs	½ tsp. salt
1 cup ground beef-kidney suet	2½ cups dry bread crumbs

Pack into a well-buttered pudding mold. Tie a doubled piece of linen or muslin over top of mold. Steam for 2 hours. Invert on serving plate, garnish with a sprig of rosemary, and serve with lemon sauce in a silver sauceboat.

LEMON SAUCE FOR FIGGY PUDDING

½ cup sugar	Juice and grated rind of
⅓ cup butter	1 lemon
1 egg	4 Tbs. boiling water
½ tsp. nutmeg	

In the top of a double boiler, cream butter and sugar, beat in egg, add nutmeg and juice and rind of lemon. Add water, slowly. Cook, stirring constantly, until thick.

Portrait—Hannah Davis

BONNETS AND BANDBOXES

MANY a ship putting into the busy ports of young America carried as a part of its exciting cargo articles of extreme interest to the girls and women waiting ashore. The arrival of silks and satins, buttons and bows, fringes and braids from ports of the Far East and of Europe was watched for eagerly by the housewives and gentlewomen of the new country. There was nurtured a love of rich and gay fashions among women, and children as well, which lasts to this day.

Among these treasures, bonnets of straw and of silks and velvets were always coveted. One fortunate—or rich—enough to own the latest fashion in bonnets was the envy of all who knew or saw her. The beautiful and intricate straw bonnets of the day were made principally in Italy and because they were so expensive, and therefore available to so few, it was not long until girls in this country were attempting to copy the straw braiding and fashioning of the imported bonnets. The first patent issued in America to a woman is said to have been recorded in 1821 for making straw bonnets of the native spear grass and red-top grass found in nearly every New England township. Abigail Adams was one of the first to own and wear such a bonnet, and her husband, the President, was very proud. From this time, native straw was braided and bonnets were made in many New England villages and towns, and local historical societies often show the results in their collections of early costumes.

Equaling the beauty of the bonnets during this era was the container in which every bonnet must be kept to be properly and fashionably protected. Bandboxes seem to have been used from quite early times in this country for storing and transporting bonnets and other articles of clothing or trinkets. It was the fashion for ladies to carry these boxes with them when they went visiting by stagecoach much as we carry traveling bags today. When taken on journeys, the bandboxes were often enclosed in a bag made of cotton with a drawstring at the top—for the boxes were so handsome that they in turn had to be protected.

During the late eighteenth and early nineteenth century, bandboxes were made in a number of places. They were generally made of thin curved wood sliced from a log, in such a way that it resembled a heavy veneer; sometimes they were made of heavy pasteboard. They were then covered with colorful papers, the first ones with hand-blocked decorative wallpapers, later with printed papers.

During this same period, in the remote southwest corner of New Hampshire, a small village to be called Jaffrey was being founded and built by sturdy pioneers, among them a certain John Eaton, who soon was an important man in the community, respected by his fellow townsmen and most useful to all, as he was a versatile master of many trades. He helped build the new homes and tradition says that he stood on his head on the ridgepole of the Christopher Wren Meeting House in Jaffrey the day he helped complete it, which was quite a feat in itself. John Eaton's daughter married another skillful workman, Peter Davis, who made wooden clocks and cheese boxes. He also had some unfortunate characteristics, and when he died left his wife and his daughter Hannah, then a young woman, without any means.

The ingenuity and skills Hannah had inherited from her father and her grandfather were not lost on the young woman. Faced with the necessity of making a living, she turned for an idea to something she knew first-hand, the making of wooden boxes somewhat in the manner of the cheese boxes her father had made.

Hannah was a pleasant girl and well liked in the town, where her cheerful disposition and helpful ways were appreciated. When it became necessary to call on friends and neighbors, she had no difficulty in eliciting their help to establish her business. For she had firmly decided that her livelihood was to be derived from the making and selling of the colorful and useful bandboxes so popular among the ladies of her time.

Hannah's method of manufacturing was entirely her own. First she searched the woods around Jaffrey for spruce trees of exactly the right size and condition, and arranged with the owner of the tree for its purchase. She then hired a man to cut the tree and haul it to her house, where it was cut into the proper lengths. For the next step, Hannah herself invented a machine which was operated by the foot-power of a strong man; a sharp blade neatly shaved the upended spruce lengths into thin vertical slices about an eighth of an inch thick. Each piece of wood thus produced was used in the manufacture of the boxes; nothing was wasted. The large pieces which were called scabboards, or scabbards, produced the body of the boxes; the smaller, narrower pieces were utilized in making smaller boxes and the rim of the box tops. The scabboards were curved into an oval shape while still green, and nailed firmly in place. The top and bottom of each box was made from a thin flat piece of pine, cut to fit the oval shape of the scabboard or side.

When the box thus fashioned was dry and completed, Hannah covered it on the outside with wallpaper which her neighbors saved for her, and she lined it with newspapers also provided by the neighbors. The dates and contents of some of these papers are a great part of the interest of the bandboxes. It is probable that, the neighbors' supplies being depleted, Hannah sometimes bought the paper, or she may very well have exchanged some of her boxes for materials, as she also bartered for many of her household needs with the storekeepers and peddlers.

When enough of the bandboxes were completed and ready to be sold, Hannah Davis would hire a gentle horse from a neighbor and hitch it to a covered wagon which she owned. Filling the wagon with her wares, she then would undertake long, tiring, and rough drives to the mill towns of the area as far away as Lowell, Massachusetts, where she was greeted with affection and eagerness by the mill girls who bought her goods. In the winter she used a sleigh for delivering her wares, and surely she was a picturesque and welcome lady Santa Claus to many who could put their new Christmas bonnets and finery into a charming and colorful Hannah Davis bandbox. A trick which she well knew would guarantee a sellout of her stock was to reach the gates of the mills at noontime on payday.

The warmhearted spinster lady was a charter member of the Baptist Church which was founded in her town and deeply devoted to it. In later years when she was unable to work because of a broken hip, the church members repaid her devotion by looking after her, and even built a cottage for her which was thereafter her home. She was loved alike by children, to whom she enjoyed telling stories of her childhood, and by grown-ups, to whom she had always been such a kindly neighbor. After her death at the age of seventy-nine, she was buried in the town she loved so much in sight of Mount Monadnock, which had been watching over her beneficently all her life, and in later years some of the young people of her beloved church dedicated a church window in her memory.

A year or two ago one of the smallest of her labeled bandboxes, about eight inches in width, was sold at a country auction in New Hampshire, after spirited bidding, for nearly thirty dollars. This little box was probably priced at twelve cents when Hannah made and sold it to an eager customer who may have used it as a trinket or jewel box. Larger bandboxes then sold for fifty cents. Each Hannah Davis bandbox can be identified by its neatly printed label pasted inside the top cover.

Warranted Nailed
BAND BOXES
Manufactured by
HANNAH DAVIS
East Jaffrey, N. H.

These bandboxes are assuredly collectors' items today. They can still be found in fair to good condition at antique shops and auctions, where they are bought mostly by museums and by the owners of old-fashioned houses where they rest underneath or atop highboys exactly as they did when they were used a hundred years or more ago. They are gay reminders of a day long gone when ladies always wore bonnets.

There are some who wonder of what use these bandboxes can be today. Their decorative value is use enough. They are also fond keepsakes of the gentle spinster known in Jaffrey, New Hampshire, as "Aunt Hannah," who so popularized bandboxes with their designs of pineapples, birds, flowers, and farm and historical scenes that her name is a New England collectors' household word a hundred years after she lived.

While angels sing, with holy mirth.
A glad New Year to all the earth.

Index